PART 1

The Backdrop

SHARON JAYNES

HARVEST HOUSE PUBLISHERS
EUGENE, OREGON

Bible translations quoted in this book can be found at end of the book.

Cover design by Leah Beachy
Cover Photo © Lisima / Creative Market
Interior design by KUHN Design Group

For bulk, special sales, or ministry purchases, please call 1-800-547-8979.
Email: Customerservice@hhpbooks.com

M is a federally registered trademark of the Hawkins Children's LLC. Harvest House Publishers, Inc., is the exclusive licensee of the trademark.

This book is a revised edition of How Jesus Broke the Rules to Set You Free *by Sharon Jaynes, previously titled* What God Really Thinks About Women.

Never Less Than
Copyright © 2015 by Sharon Jaynes
Published by Harvest House Publishers
Eugene, Oregon 97408
www.harvesthousepublishers.com

ISBN 978-0-7369-8285-6 (pbk)
ISBN 978-0-7369-8286-3 (eBook)

LCCN Number: 2021937795

Printed in the United States of America

21 22 23 24 25 26 27 28 29 / BP / 10 9 8 7 6 5 4 3 2 1

Contents

CHAPTER 1

The Worth of a Woman

She was beautiful.

She was bright.

And she was mad at God.

I sat across the lunch table, picking at a salad and trying to digest Jan's words.

"I don't understand God. It seems like He's against women. He's set us up to fail. Even our bodies are weaker, and that just invites men to abuse us. All through the Bible I see how God used men in mighty ways. Abraham, Moses, David—you name it; it's always the men. And polygamy. How could God allow that? Today, there's so much abuse toward women. Where's God in all that? There are so many inequalities and injustices between how men are treated and how women are treated. What kind of God does that? I think the bottom line is that God just doesn't like women."

Jan knew her Bible. She grew up in church, had loving Christian parents, and accepted Christ when she was eight years old. "I accepted Jesus because I was afraid of hell," Jan confessed. "It wasn't because I had discovered a loving God who cared about me. I did it because of fear."

Regardless of why Jan became a Christian, her decision was real. She continued growing in her little-girl faith, and she even felt a call to ministry when she was in the eighth grade. She truly had a heart for the things of God.

But all during her growing-up years, Jan felt she wasn't as valuable or competent as her male counterparts. She saw herself as less than her younger brother, and she felt that her parents favored him over her. "They always paid more attention to my brother," she explained. "And if we got into a fight, my parents took his side. 'Leave your brother alone,' they'd say. But I never heard, 'Leave your sister alone.'"

As is often the case with children, Jan's perception of her earthly father colored her perception of her heavenly Father, and the idea of male favoritism became the sieve through which her spiritual interpretations passed.

Jan graduated from high school with honors, from college with a degree in communication studies, and from seminary with a degree in theology. "When I got to seminary and started reading about some of the ancient philosophers' opinions of women, as well as some of the early church fathers', and even some modern-day theologians', I just got mad. The more I read, the madder I got. Is it true? Are women less than men? Does God favor one gender over the other?"

When I met Jan, she was a 26-year-old seminary graduate, working as a secretary in a growing church. As she considered her role as a woman in ministry, she couldn't find any role models. She was frustrated, confused, and, as I mentioned earlier, just plain mad.

We talked for hours, and we have talked many more hours since then. Jan brought up some valid questions. She was brave enough to voice what many women feel, and we struggled with her questions together. I know what it's like to be in Jan's place of frustration, but in the two decades plus that I've journeyed to answer those questions, God has opened my eyes to witness what He truly thinks about women.

In my early adult years, I was very happy in my ignorance and limited understanding of the roles and responsibilities of women in the body of Christ. But God wouldn't allow me to remain comfortable in my shallow understanding of His deep love and multifaceted plan for women.

For far too long I looked at women in the Bible through the wrong end of the telescope, making them appear much too small in comparison to their male counterparts. But God kept needling me to take a closer look. Through the years I've asked a lot of questions, read many respected theologians' interpretations and opinions, and examined more Greek and Hebrew words of Scripture than this Southern girl knew existed. But I just kept coming back to Jesus' ministry, miracles, and messages. I asked God how He really felt about women, and He showed me through the life of His Son. When Philip asked Jesus to show him the Father, Jesus answered, "Anyone who has seen me has seen the Father" (John 14:9). The writer of Hebrews describes Jesus as "the exact representation of [God's] being" (Hebrews 1:3). And while I don't presume to know the mind of God, I can understand His character and His ways through the ministry of Jesus, His Son.

God spoke audibly to Jesus two times in the Gospels. God said, "This is my Son, whom I love; with him I am well pleased," after Jesus' baptism recorded in Matthew 3:17. And again, at the mount of transfiguration, God said, "This is my Son, whom I love; with him I am well pleased." Then He added, "Listen to him!" (Matthew 17:5). So I have been trying to do just that: listen to Him.

As we turn the page from Malachi 4:6 to Matthew 1:1, God breaks 400 years of silence, and we get a hint that a new day is on the horizon. In the Old Testament genealogies, families were traced through the males only. However, in the genealogy of Jesus Christ, the rhythm of "the father of, the father of, the father of," comes to a screeching halt as a woman's name appears on the page: "Zerah, whose mother was Tamar" (Matthew 1:3). Then the usual cadence picks right back up where it left off with "the father of, the father of, the father of." Once again, the harmonious flow is abruptly arrested with "Boaz, whose mother was Rahab, Boaz the father of Obed, whose mother was Ruth" (Matthew 1:5). Altogether, five women are listed in this genealogy: Tamar, Rahab, Ruth, Bathsheba, and Mary. The fact that they were listed at all is reason for pause.

God was up to something. It was time for the female image bearers to come out of the shadows and into the light. And that light is the light of Christ.

In God's infinite wisdom, He has given us many ways to learn of His character and His ways. We learn of Him through His Word, through creation, and most of all through His Son. Eugene Peterson paraphrases John 14:9-10 this way: "To see me is to see the Father... The words that I speak to you aren't mere words. I don't just make them up on my own. The Father who resides in me crafts each word into a divine act" (MSG).

Jesus spoke exactly what the Father told Him to speak and did exactly what His Father told Him to do. He was the "image of the invisible God" and "the exact representation of His being." By observing Jesus' treatment *of* women, we discover God's love *toward* women. He called women out of the shadows of society and placed them center stage. We can consider this freedom in two ways: freedom *from* and freedom *to*.

- Jesus came to liberate women *from* centuries of oppressions that told them they were less than. He set them free *to* impact God's kingdom and the world—a freedom that has not been duplicated in any other religion.

- Jesus set women free *from* the culture's view that females were less than their male counterparts, freeing them *to* step out of the shadows to be integrated as valuable members of God's family.

- He set women free *from* being sequestered in their homes and set them free *to* go out into the world to tell the Good News of Christ.

In a culture that kept women tucked away in the recesses of the home to be neither seen nor heard, Jesus pulled them from behind the scenes, positioned them front and center, and shone on them the spotlight of His divine love and calling. As the curtain of the New Testament rises, women fill the stage and take starring roles as God's grand drama of redemption unfolds.

Jesus called women out of the shadows of
society and placed them center stage.

Jesus made deliberate choices in the *who, what, when,* and *where* of His teachings and miracles. It was no accident that many of His healings occurred on the Sabbath. It was no accident that many of His conversations were with women. It was no accident that women were the recipients of many of His miraculous healings. It was no accident that the culture's "least of these" received the best of Him.

Paul wrote, "There is neither Jew nor Gentile, neither slave nor free, nor is there male and female, for you are all one in Christ Jesus" (Galatians 3:28). Sometimes we humans can take a simple message and make it very complicated. But the Word couldn't be more clear: There is no "less than" in the body of Christ or in the world at large. Jesus valued and validated women throughout His ministry in ways that astonished those within earshot and left slack-jawed those within eyeshot.

What I saw, and what you're going to see, is that Jesus crossed man-made social, political, racial, and gender boundaries to address women with the respect due image bearers of God. But before we begin our journey of walking in these women's sandals, we need to grasp the darkened world into which Jesus stepped—the backdrop for God's redemptive plan for women to unfold.

> By observing Jesus' treatment of women,
> we discover God's love toward women.

IN THE BEGINNING...

When Jesus entered the world on that starry night in Bethlehem, His first cry echoed the heart cries of women who had been misused and abused for centuries. By the time Jesus took His first steps onto the dusty ground of Galilee, women were not allowed to talk to men in public, testify in court, or mingle with men at social gatherings. They were considered sensual temptresses and the chief causes of sexual sin. Women were considered a "lower animal species."[1] Men divorced their wives on a whim and tossed them out like burned bread. Women lived in the shadows of society, rarely seen and seldom heard. Much like a slave, a girl was the property of her father and if married, the property of her husband. Women were uneducated, unappreciated, and uncounted.

How did this happen? When and where did such a low regard of women begin? Certainly this was not God's intent.

It all began in the Garden of Eden.

"In the beginning God created the heavens and the earth" (Genesis 1:1). Before the creation of the world, there was nothing. Then God spoke the world into existence. He said, "Let there be," and it was so. God hung the sun and moon and then sprinkled stars about the expanse. He separated the dry ground from the seas and stocked both with vegetation and wildlife galore. Then, on the sixth day, God said, "Let us make mankind in our image, in our likeness, so that they may rule over the fish in the sea and the birds in the sky, over the livestock and all the wild animals, and over all the creatures that move along the ground" (Genesis 1:26).

> The Lord God formed a man from the dust of the ground and breathed into his nostrils the breath of life, and the man became a living being (Genesis 2:7).

After each of the first five days of creation, as the sun set over the horizon, God said, "It is good." Six times, at the end of each phase of His handiwork, He reiterated His approval. We ride the rhythm of repetition only to be brought to a sudden halt by the Creator's words when He looked at the lone man with no suitable companion: "It is *not* good for the man to be alone" (Genesis 2:18, emphasis mine).

And while God knew that it was not good for the man to be alone, He waited for Adam to come to that conclusion himself.

> Now the Lord God had formed out of the ground all the wild animals and all the birds in the sky. He brought them to the man to see what he would name them; and whatever the man called each living creature, that was its name. So the man gave names to all the livestock, the birds in the sky and all the wild animals. But for Adam no suitable helper was found (Genesis 2:19-20).

Can't you just see Adam watching the animals prancing and flitting about, two by two, male and female? The bright-red male cardinal and his demure, grayish songbird. The bushy-faced lion and his sleek, adoring lioness. The udder-dangling bovine and her fiery-eyed bull. Longingly, Adam observes the pairs of God's creation nuzzling, cuddling, and frolicking about. And while he was surrounded by noisy creatures and a loving God, Adam realized, in a sense, that he was all alone.

Adam's aloneness must have grown with each pair of animals that filed by to accept their name tags. *What about me?* he might have mused as the last two creatures took flight. Oh, my friend, the best was yet to come!

> The LORD God caused the man to fall into a deep sleep; and while he was sleeping, he took one of the man's ribs and then closed up the place with flesh. Then the LORD God made a woman from the rib he had taken out of the man (Genesis 2:21-22).

Bruce Marchiano paints a beautiful picture for us.

> He shapes her frame and shades her skin. He molds her mind and measures her structure. He sculpts the contour of her face, the almonds of her eyes, and the graceful stretch of her limbs. Long before she has even spoken a word, he has held her voice in his heart, and so he ever so gently tunes its timbre. Cell by cell, tenderness by tenderness, and with care beyond care, in creation he quite simply loves her.[2]

When Adam woke from his God-induced sleep, he took one look at the fair Eve and I imagine he said, "Now *this* is good!" We don't know exactly what Adam's first words were when he initially laid eyes on Eve, but we do know his first recorded utterance when she came into view.

> This is now bone of my bones and flesh of my flesh; she shall be called "woman," for she was taken out of man (Genesis 2:23).

What a beautiful portrait of Jesus' promise, "Your Father knows what you need before you ask him" (Matthew 6:8). Yes, God knows what we need and often waits until we realize it before He provides. Had He created Adam and Eve simultaneously, Adam would have never known just how much he needed her.

Eve was the "crowning touch of God's creative masterpiece and the inspiration of man's first poetry."[3] Woman was not an afterthought, but God's grand finale. Eve was not less than Adam, but part of a whole created to complete the picture of God's image bearer. Man could not do it alone. Woman could not do it alone. Both were necessary—working, serving, and living in tandem to complete what God intended all along.

God concluded the first week of the world's existence, and the curtain fell with the words, "God saw all that he had made, and it was *very* good" (Genesis 1:31, emphasis mine). With the debut of woman, what was "good" now became "very good."

> Woman was not an afterthought, but God's
> grand finale. Eve was not less than Adam,
> but part of a whole created to complete
> the picture of God's image bearer.

GOD CREATED AN *EZER*

So who is this woman and why was she created? Like two pieces of a puzzle, Eve was created to complete man. C.S. Lewis paints a beautiful picture:

> The Christian idea of marriage is based on Christ's words that a man and wife are to be regarded as a single organism—for that is what the words "one flesh" would be in modern English. And the Christians believe that when He said this He was not expressing a sentiment but stating a

fact—just as one is stating a fact when one says that a lock and its key are one mechanism, or that a violin and a bow are one musical instrument. The inventor of the human machine was telling us that its two halves, the male and the female, were made to be combined together in pairs, not simply on the sexual level, but totally combined.[4]

Like a violin without a bow, or a lock without a key, man was incomplete without woman. Together, they were whole.

The Bible tells us Eve was created to be Adam's helper. It is the word *helper* that has caused much discussion and debate over the years, so let's address that right from the start. The Greek word for *helper* can also be translated "partner."

While some women may bristle at the thought of being called a mere "helper," we need only to look at the pages of Scripture to see that "helper" holds a place of great honor. The Hebrew word "helper" that is used for woman is *ezer.* It is derived from the Hebrew word used of God and the Holy Spirit, *azar.* Both mean "helper"—one who comes alongside to aid or assist. King David wrote, "Lord, be my help" (Psalm 30:10). "The Lord is with me; he is my helper" (Psalm 118:7). Moses said of God, "My father's God was my helper; he saved me from the sword of Pharaoh" (Exodus 18:4).

Ezer appears 21 times in the Old Testament. Two times it is used of the woman in Genesis 2, 16 times it is used of God or Yahweh as the helper of His people. The remaining three references appear in the books of the prophets, who use it in reference to military aid.

Bible scholar Dr. Victor P. Hamilton explains:

> The new creation (woman) will be neither a superior nor an inferior, but an equal. The creation of this helper will form one-half of a polarity, and will be to man as the south pole is the north pole...Any suggestion that this particular word denotes one who has only an associate or subordinate

status to a senior member is refuted by the fact that most frequently this same word describes Yahweh's relationship to Israel. He is Israel's help(er).[5]

Whatever we may believe about a woman's roles and responsibilities, it is clear that man's decided aloneness was a dilemma that needed divine attention. Woman is introduced as a partner in vocation, procreation, and relational habitation. Together they shared a common calling—to fill, subdue, and rule the earth. Yes, their roles and responsibilities may have been different. Our physical bodies would dictate such. But as far as being an image bearer of God, there was no distinction drawn at creation.

Now, don't get me wrong. I love serving my husband and taking care of his needs. Strange as it may seem, I even enjoy cleaning the house! But those duties do not define the word *ezer*. In fact, the beauty of the word *ezer* or "helper" is that God didn't define what that was to look like. He didn't write out male and female job descriptions or give Adam and Eve a list of prescribed duties. God said to both of them, "Be fruitful and increase in number; fill the earth and subdue it. Rule over the fish of the sea and the birds in the sky and over every living creature that moves on the ground" (Genesis 1:28). Adam didn't say to Eve, "You take the birds and I'll take the fish." They ruled and subdued together.

There is nothing more beautiful than a husband and wife who have truly "become one flesh" and entered into the symbiotic dance of marriage, moving as one to the tune of God's love and the rhythm of His will—working together to be God's image bearers in the world.

But what about the woman who is not married? Is she an *ezer* as well? Absolutely! Woman was created to be a helper and rescuer no matter what her marital status in life. I was just as much God's warrior in the spiritual kingdom when I was single as I am today.

Each of the sixteen times *ezer* is used in reference to God as our

Helper, it also carries military connotations. Even the Proverbs 31 woman—the woman who has been held up as a godly role model for centuries—was referred to in military terms. "An excellent wife, who can find?" the passage begins. The Hebrew word that is translated "excellent" or "virtuous" can also mean "wealthy, prosperous, valiant, boldly courageous, powerful, mighty warrior."

Did you catch that? "Mighty warrior." Consider Paul's words to the churches in Ephesus and Corinth that encourage us to stand in the spiritual battle as praying men and women armed with God's Word:

> Finally, be strong in the Lord and in his mighty power. Put on the full armor of God, so that you can take your stand against the devil's schemes. For our struggle is not against flesh and blood, but against the rulers, against the authorities, against the powers of this dark world and against the spiritual forces of evil in the heavenly realms (Ephesians 6:10-12).

> Though we live in the world, we do not wage war as the world does. The weapons we fight with are not the weapons of the world. On the contrary, they have divine power to demolish strongholds. We demolish arguments and every pretension that sets itself up against the knowledge of God, and we take captive every thought to make it obedient to Christ (2 Corinthians 10:3-5).

God didn't create woman simply because man was lonely, even though that was obviously the case. He created woman to complete man—to love with him, work with him, rule with him, live with him, procreate with him, and fight alongside him. She was a female image bearer in this mysterious union of marriage. Woman was and is a warrior called to fight alongside man in the greatest battle that was yet to come—a battle not fought on the battlefield with guns, but on our knees in prayer.

Why have I gone into such great length about this word *ezer*? Because, dear friend, I want you to grasp the full impact of what

God created you to be. You are an amazing masterpiece fashioned by Almighty God. You are a woman.

AFTER THE FALL

So what happened? How did woman move from a mutual place of honor as image bearer in the Garden of Eden to a burden bearer moving in the shadows of the cultures that followed? Well, let's not leave the garden just yet.

Chapter 3 of Genesis begins with these daunting words: "Now the serpent…" Satan was not happy about these image bearers God had created. Even though he had once been an angel of light, Satan had been cast to the earth with one-third of the angels because of their rebellion against God (Revelation 12:4). He knew he was doomed and wanted to take as many of God's image bearers with him as possible. So he started with the first two.

We don't have clear evidence as to why Satan engaged Eve in conversation regarding eating the forbidden fruit, but we do know that Adam stood passively by as the drama unfolded. Even though Genesis 3 states that Satan addressed "the woman," he used the Hebrew plural form of "you" when he spoke. He wasn't just talking to her.

Some say that the sin began when Eve tried to get the upper hand in the relationship, but there was no upper hand to gain. Adam and Eve lived in harmony with each other. They moved as one. If she had been trying to get the upper hand, then she would have kept the fruit to herself and not offered it to her husband as well.

Some say Adam sinned because he listened to his wife. But Eve wasn't created to be a silent partner. It wasn't that he listened to her as a woman, but that he listened to what she said and ate the fruit.[6]

In the end, both believed Satan's lies and disobeyed God. Consequently, sin and shame entered the world, and their harmonious relationship with God and each other was broken. Adam and Eve sewed fig leaf aprons in an effort to cover their shame and crouched behind the bushes in an effort to hide from God.

But then, in the cool of the evening, God strolled through the Garden and asked, "Where are you?" The first recorded question in the Bible was not man questioning God, but God pursuing man (Genesis 3:9). That is the question He still asks today as He pursues humankind to restore what was broken with that first act of disobedience. "Where are you?" God wasn't asking because He didn't know where they were, but He was calling them out in the open to confront their sin and explain the consequences to come.

The serpent, the woman, and the man were all judged, but only the serpent and the ground were cursed. In Genesis 3:15, God said the offspring of a woman would crush the serpent's head and the serpent would strike his heel. That might seem like an odd verse, but God isn't just talking about snakes. He's talking about the devil himself—and about the offspring of a woman defeating the devil once and for all. All along, it was God's redemptive plan for the Savior of the world to be born of a woman. God certainly didn't have to do it that way, but He chose to use a woman in the unfolding of salvation's plan. Satan clearly understood that his demise would come from a woman's womb. And from the very beginning, he has tried to destroy her.

Previously, Adam and Eve ruled together, but all that was about to change. To Eve God said, "Your desire will be for your husband, and he will rule over you" (verse 16). From that time on, relational tension between man and woman was the new reality.

But the good news is that God had a plan to make all that went wrong in the Garden of Eden right again in the Garden of Gethsemane. While the tree in the garden brought spiritual death and the curse, the tree of Calvary brought spiritual life and blessing. Jesus came to set the captive free. He came to destroy the works of the devil (1 John 3:8). But thousands of years were sandwiched between God's words about Jesus, "He will," and our Savior's words, "I have." And in the meantime, women have been devalued, defiled, and degraded in every way imaginable.

BETWEEN THE GARDEN OF EDEN AND THE GARDEN OF GETHSEMANE

Many years passed before God's kingdom calendar signaled that Jesus' redemptive plan was to begin. In order to grasp just how radically liberating Jesus' actions and teachings were for women, we need to understand the world Jesus stepped into. Now, don't let me lose you here. This next section is a bit academic, and I promise the rest of the book will not feel like a history lesson. But we need to understand how women went from being God's final masterpiece at creation to being viewed as insignificant shadows at Jesus' incarnation. We can't fully understand how radically freeing Jesus' actions were toward women until we understand how culturally bound they were.

Much of the ancient world was influenced by philosophers and their teachings. For most of us, ancient philosophy might not have much impact on our day-to-day lives, but in the fifth century BC, it affected the entire culture. It was the philosophers' teaching and influence that shackled women and kept them in bondage to a patriarchal society. For example, in ancient Athens, a city named after the beautiful goddess of wisdom, philosophers held to the belief that women were inferior to men on every level. These philosophers created the lens through which much of the civilized world looked at life. Socrates (470–399 BC) argued that being born a woman was a divine punishment, since a woman is halfway between a man and an animal.[7] Respectable Greek wives led secluded lives and rarely appeared in social situations. They took no part in public affairs and rarely appeared at meals or social occasions to mingle with the men.[8]

Socrates taught Plato, who believed that women were a "degenerate form of manly perfection," and that men who did not live righteous lives would be reincarnated as females.[9] He believed this is how the entire female gender came into existence.[10]

Plato passed his teaching along to Aristotle, who declared, "The courage of a man is shown in commanding, of a woman in obeying."[11] He taught that women were inferior and needed to be commanded by men and used for their pleasure. Men who were serious about their studies were encouraged to avoid women altogether, as women were considered a distraction and temptation. Aristotle observed the nature of bees and noted how the swarm was led by one apparent leader, which he assumed was the "king bee." It would be centuries before naturalists discovered the leader was indeed a "queen bee." (You go, girl.)

Demosthenes, who was a noted orator during Aristotle's day, stated that the role of Athenian women was as follows: "We have courtesans for our pleasures, prostitutes [that is, young female slaves] for daily physical use, wives to bring up legitimate children and to be faithful stewards in household matters."[12]

The ancients believed that life came from a man's semen, where tiny human beings were stored. Women simply served as the soil in which the seed was planted and allowed to grow until birth. They knew nothing of a woman's eggs and only drew conclusions from what their naked eyes could see. It wasn't until the 1800s that scientists discovered women had eggs. Before that, women were thought of as holding tanks. It makes sense that if women are thought of as the "dirt" into which the seeds are planted, then they will be treated like dirt as well.

The Romans didn't view women quite as harshly as the Greeks, but they still believed that women needed to be kept under men's control.[13] The Romans were more progressive as to what activities a woman could engage in outside the home, but her reach wasn't far from her front door. If a woman was caught in adultery, Roman law gave the husband the right to kill her because she was his property. However, a man could have sexual relations outside of marriage at will. Roman men tended to share the Greek view of women as either objects of pleasure or sources of temptation.[14]

These ancient philosophers were bright men who were darkly deceived. It would be very easy to raise our ire against the philosophers of the past, or even those in Middle Eastern countries who continue to treat women with the same disdain today, but I always go back to the source. It is the devil himself who seeks to kill, steal, and destroy (John 10:10).

In the Jewish culture, women were not treated much better than their Roman and Greek sisters. Even though the Old Testament is filled with influential women—such as Deborah the prophetess, who advised military leaders; Esther the queen, who saved the Jews from annihilation; Rahab the prostitute, who rescued the spies from soldiers of Jericho; and Abigail the farmer's wife, who stopped King David's needless assassination plan, just to name a few—women were still considered a commodity.

The Jewish people became more integrated with and influenced by foreign cultures that oppressed women. By the time Jesus was born, Jewish women were not allowed to talk to a man in public…even to their husbands. If a woman spoke to a man in public who was not her husband, it was assumed she was having a relationship with him—and her actions constituted grounds for divorce. Women were not allowed to eat in the same room with a gathering of men, to be educated in the Torah (the Scriptures) with men, or to enter the inner court of the temple to worship with men. Two thousand years ago, Rabbi Eliezer stated, "Rather should the words of the Torah be burned than entrusted to a woman!"[15]

A rabbi might not even speak to his own daughter or sister in public. Some Pharisees were referred to as "the bruised and bleeding ones" because they would shut their eyes upon seeing a woman on the street, causing them to walk into walls and houses.[16] Each morning a Pharisee began his day by thanking God that He had not made him a "Gentile, a woman, or a slave."[17]

A woman was considered the property of her father. That ownership was passed to her husband when she married and to her son when she was widowed. There was little hope for a woman devoid of all three. Women were considered the dregs of society and were thought to be responsible for much of the evil in the world. They were segregated in the social and religious life of their communities and considered inferior, unteachable creatures whose sole purposes were for domesticity and a man's sexual pleasure.[18]

I could say more, but I think this is enough to allow us to catch a glimpse of how women were viewed and why. It was ugly. It was dark. It was oppressive. That is the world Jesus stepped into. That is the backdrop for God's ultimate drama of redemption to unfold.

Why did Jesus come to earth? John tells us in a nutshell: "The reason the Son of God appeared was to destroy the devil's work" (1 John 3:8). Jesus came to restore God's original design for men and women as co–image bearers that began its downfall in the garden. He came to restore fallen humanity in every sense of the word. Part of that restoration included restoring Eve to the position she enjoyed before the fall. Jesus walked on the scene to see God's female image bearers hidden in the shadows behind lock and key, and He flung the doors open wide.

It is easy for us of the twenty-first century to view Jesus' interactions with women as somewhat ordinary, but the God-made-man broke a man-made rule every single time He interacted with a woman in the New Testament. Jesus was so far out on a limb, it was a good thing He made the tree. When we understand a bit of the Roman and Greek philosophy and treatment of women at the time Jesus appeared on the earth, we can better understand just how radical Jesus' treatment of women really was. He took these devalued and degraded female image bearers and placed them center stage to play leading roles in God's redemptive plan.

Now, let's walk the well-worn paths with Jesus and discover how He surprised the world by the way He interacted with women.

The God-made-man broke a man-made
rule every single time He interacted with
a woman in the New Testament.

PART 2

Jesus Calling Women Center Stage

CHAPTER 2

Chosen

Just an Ordinary Girl

Traveling down the dusty road to Bethlehem on the lumpy back-bone of a donkey was hard enough, but being jostled along while nine-months pregnant was unbearably painful. The two blankets Joseph had placed over the hairy beast did little to cushion the rough ride for his young bride and mother-to-be.

"How are you faring?" a concerned Joseph asked.

"I just hope this baby is more comfortable than I am," Mary breathed. "I don't think He's going to wait much longer."

Mary placed her free hand on her mounding abdomen. *Who would have ever thought the Savior of the world would spend His final moments in my womb riding on the back of a donkey? Who would have ever thought the Messiah would be born to a girl like me?* Her thoughts went back to the day the angel Gabriel appeared to her and announced God's redemptive plan.

"Mary," her mother had called. "Are you finished kneading the dough? Don't forget to milk the goat. And then there's the robe that is half finished. It seems our work is never done!"

At 15, Mary had a full schedule of daily activities simply keeping the home running smoothly. But soon enough it would no longer be her father's house she served, but her husband's. The marriage between her and Joseph had been arranged since she was a child, but that did not diminish romantic notions of being swept away in the middle of the night by her handsome groom. Their engagement was a legally binding contract, and all that remained were the technicalities—the actual wedding celebration.

If all goes well, I will be married to Joseph within a year's time. But then, what could go wrong? The contract has been signed, the bride-price has been paid, and the room connected to his father's house is almost complete.

As the young maiden continued daydreaming about her new life, a golden presence filled the room. The hair on the back of her neck bristled as a gentle breeze brushed her cheek. The window remained fastened while an indescribable stirring swirled around her. Looking up from her work, she was startled by the glowing figure standing before her.

A single gasp filled her lungs as Mary clasped her hand over her mouth. Wide eyes tried to make sense of the vision before her. Was it a man? A ghost? An angel? Was she dreaming?

"Greetings, highly favored one! The Lord is with you."

Seeing her pale before him, the angel Gabriel continued, "Do not be afraid, Mary. You have found favor with God. I have come to tell you that you will be with child and will give birth to a son, and you shall name Him Jesus. This is all God's plan for you and for Him. He will be great and will be called the Son of the Most High. God will give Him the throne of His father David, and He will reign over the house of Jacob forever. In other words, His kingdom will never end."

A son? Pregnant? Jesus? Son of the Most High? A jumble of thoughts spilled out all at once as she tried to piece together the information lying like scattered puzzle pieces before her.

"How can this be? I am still a virgin."

Gabriel leaned in and held Mary's gaze. "The power of the Most

High, through the Holy Spirit, will make this happen. The Holy One you will bear will be called the Son of God."

Sensing her bewildered and troubled heart, the messenger knew she needed a bit more assurance. She needed a friend. He leaned back and remarked, "That's not all. Your cousin Elizabeth, who is way past her fertile years and thought to be barren, is also pregnant. She's in her sixth month already. See, nothing is impossible with God."

With that reminder of God's omnipotent power, Mary embraced her calling. "May it be to me as you have said."

Then, just as quickly and quietly as he had appeared, the angel was gone.

Mary stood alone in the room trying to take in all that had happened. A swarm of questions circled her mind. "I've got to get to Elizabeth," Mary whispered.

Right away, Mary packed a few articles of clothing and began her 80-mile journey from Nazareth to Judea. After nine days, she arrived.

As soon as Mary entered the room, Elizabeth was filled with the Holy Spirit and began prophesying. In a loud voice she proclaimed: "Blessed are you among women, and blessed is the child you will bear! But why am I so favored, that the mother of my Lord should come to me? As soon as the sound of your greeting reached my ears, the baby in my womb leapt for joy. Blessed is she who has believed that what the Lord has said to her will be accomplished!"

CHOSEN TO CARRY

What an amazing encounter for one so young. God's plan of redemption was held by the thread of a teenage girl from Nazareth. Who knew it would be so strong?

We don't know exactly how old Mary was at the time of Gabriel's proclamation. Commentaries have suggested anywhere between 13 and 16—marrying age during that time in history.

Nazareth was considered an insignificant town, yet God used it in a significant way. Likewise, Mary was a seemingly insignificant girl, yet God chose her for a significant role in the most important story of all time. Her selfless surrender serves as an example of the impact that obedience to God's call can have on our lives and on the lives of others as well.

Let's go to the actual Scripture and take a closer look.

Greetings, you who are highly favored! (Luke 1:28).

Why Mary? Why that particular girl? What was it about her that caused God to choose her? We will never know the answers to those questions, but we can get a glimpse into God's heart by looking closely at the word *favored*.

Gabriel greeted Mary by saying she was "highly favored." When we look at the word *favored*, we realize that the choice had little to do with Mary and everything to do with God. The Greek word *charis* used in verse 28 is translated both "favor" and "grace." Grace is unmerited favor from God. It is a gift we can't earn and certainly don't deserve but are freely given simply because God wants to give it.

The Bible says we are chosen by grace (Romans 11:5-6), saved by grace (Romans 3:24), and given spiritual gifts by grace (Romans 12:6). Paul says that God lavishes His grace on us (Ephesians 1:7-8). Don't you just love that? He doesn't dole out a teaspoon here and there, but He pours out His favor on us—bathing us in His grace.

Why was Mary chosen? The same reason God chose you and me to be His children. Because of grace. We are not saved because we deserve it. She was not chosen to be the mother of Jesus because she earned it. She was chosen because of God's grace.

The Lord is with you (Luke 1:28).

For many years I began each day praying for my son: "God, please be with Steven today." Then one day God stopped me mid-prayer.

Sharon, I am with Steven every day, He seemed to say. *Why do you continue asking for something Steven already has?*

God was right! (Imagine that.) God was with Steven at all times, just as He is with you and me. He promised each of His children, "Never will I leave you; never will I forsake you" (Hebrews 13:5). After God's reminder, I changed my prayer for Steven. "God, I pray that Steven will sense Your presence in his life today. Thank You for being with him, just as You promised."

Mary needed that same reassurance. The reminder of God's presence in her life would be crucial for the news that Gabriel was about to deliver.

Do not be afraid, Mary; you have found favor with God (Luke 1:30).

If Gabriel showed up at my door, I think "do not be afraid" would be the appropriate first words. As a matter of fact, it seems as though these are some of the first words God and His messengers spoke to many called on for special assignment. "Do not be afraid," God said to Abram (Genesis 15:1). "Do not be afraid," God said to Joshua (Joshua 8:1). "Do not be afraid," the angel said to Zechariah (Luke 1:13). "Do not be afraid," the angel said to the shepherds (Luke 2:10).

And now, when God is calling an ordinary girl out of the shadows to stand center stage, He reassures her with the same courage-bolstering words. "Do not be afraid. God is with you." And if anyone was going to need reassurance of God's presence in her life, it was Mary.

Gabriel then proceeded to tell her about her God-ordained assignment. She would conceive a Son by the power of the Holy Spirit and give Him the name Jesus. *Jesus* is the Greek form of the name Joshua, which means "the Lord saves." Mary was part of this fallen world, and like all of mankind, she needed a Savior. When Paul wrote, "All have sinned and fall short of the glory of God" (Romans 3:23), that included Mary.

In Mary's own song of praise, she cried out, "My soul glorifies the

Lord and my spirit rejoices in God my Savior" (Luke 1:46-47). Regardless of what artists have painted through the centuries, Mary did not have a halo over her head. In her own words, she, just like you and me, needed a Savior. She was just an ordinary girl with an extraordinary calling.

God set the stage and called Mary of Nazareth to take her position front and center. Who would have ever imagined she would take her place with such courage?

How will this be, since I am a virgin? (Luke 1:34).

Mary's question didn't mean she doubted what the angel said was true, and her wonderment did not mean she was reluctant. She was just confused about the physiology of the process, questioning the logistics and seeking to make sense of it all. She had never slept with a man, so how was this possible?

The angel saw the purity of her heart and went on to explain exactly how this would occur. In a day when women were not formally taught the Scriptures, Mary had a front-row seat with one of God's personal messengers for private tutoring.

She was taught by Gabriel. She believed by faith. She obeyed by choice. But this heavenly decision caused an earthly dilemma. An unwed pregnancy could lead to her parents disowning her, her fiancé divorcing her, and her accusers stoning her to death. Regardless of the risks, Mary's selfless surrender takes our breath away.

I am the Lord's servant. May your word to me be fulfilled (Luke 1:38).

When God called Moses to lead the Israelites out of Egyptian captivity, Moses tried to convince Him to send someone else (Exodus 4:13). When God called Gideon to lead the Israelites into battle, Gideon reminded Him of his lack of credentials and asked for a sign (Judges 6:17). When God called Jeremiah to be the next great prophet, Jeremiah argued that he was far too young for the job (Jeremiah 1:6).

When God appointed Jonah to preach repentance to the people of Nineveh, he hopped on the next boat out of town (Jonah 1:3). But when God called Mary to bear His only Son, she accepted the assignment with beauty and grace. "I am the Lord's servant," Mary answered. "May it be to me as you have said."

In Eugene Peterson's paraphrase, *The Message*, Mary said, "Yes, I see it all now: I'm the Lord's maid, ready to serve. Let it be with me just as you say." Mary's words to embrace her calling showcase her courage.

COUSIN ELIZABETH
CALLED TO PROPHESY

I cannot leave this chapter without shining the spotlight on another chosen woman. At God's prompting, Elizabeth met Mary on the stage, grabbed her by the hand, and joined her on the journey to fulfill an extraordinary purpose. But this was not simply a supporting role. She was a leading lady in her own right.

Elizabeth was more than an incubator for the forerunner of Jesus, John the Baptist. She was a prophet chosen by God to mentor the mother of His child. Elizabeth's grasp of the situation was remarkable! She understood that the baby Mary was chosen to carry was the Messiah when even those closest to Jesus in future years would not. And why was that? Was it because she was particularly smart or insightful? No. It was because the illuminating power of the Holy Spirit revealed it to her. And that is the same with you and me. We only understand spiritual truth when the Holy Spirit opens our eyes to see.

Isn't it wonderful that God created women for relationship? He knew Mary was going to need a friend. God is always with us, but sometimes He gives us like-minded friends with whom to walk the journey. It was a new day for women, and it all began with two cousins.

After Elizabeth's prophecy, Mary became a flowing fountain of praise. Words from Scripture mingled with words from her own heart and created a chorus of wonderment and awe. And while she sang with joy, this heavenly purpose would eventually cause earthly pain.

Elizabeth said it well of Mary: "Blessed is she who has believed that what the Lord has said to her will be accomplished!" Could that be said of you? Could that be said of me? Do we believe God has chosen us for a unique purpose in a specific time and place in history? In Acts 17:26, Paul told the people of Athens that God had "marked out their appointed times in history and the boundaries of their lands." You may not have been chosen to carry a specific child such as Mary and Elizabeth, but you were chosen for God's purposes.

Jesus said this about the believers of His day and about you. "You did not choose me, but I chose you and appointed you so that you might go and bear fruit—fruit that will last—and so that whatever you ask in my name the Father will give you" (John 15:16).

Do you believe that God has chosen you, and that He will complete what He has planned for you and through you? If so, then you, my friend, are just the kind of woman God is looking for to accomplish mighty feats. Paul tells us that there is "incomparably great power for us who believe" (Ephesians 1:19).

As I mentioned before, the redemptive plan of God hung by the thread of a young Jewish girl. Mary risked everything: her reputation, her marriage, her family, her income, her dreams, and her life. She was an *ezer* who stepped out onto the battlefield, armed with faith in the One who called her. In doing so, she experienced breathtaking privilege accompanied by unspeakable pain.

Do you want to be a woman entrusted with God-sized assignments? Then memorize those words of Mary: "I am the Lord's servant. May your word to me be fulfilled." May that be the refrain to every chorus of our life's song.

CHOSEN TO FLIP THE SWITCH

It had been over 30 years since Gabriel appeared to Mary and announced the news that she was chosen to bear the Son of God. Most days, her life was just like any other Jewish mother's. Like today, for instance, the family packed up to go to a wedding.

It was a beautiful day for the ceremony. Mary only hoped the good weather would hold out for the seven days of celebration to follow. She was glad for the break in the mundane activities of running a household and looked forward to spending extended time with her son.

"I hope you don't mind if I bring along a few friends," Jesus said as He walked in from His work in the carpentry shop.

"Of course not! As long as they will behave and not embarrass the family," she teased.

Jesus turned to Mary with a look that pierced her soul. "These men have been chosen as well."

Chosen. There was that word again. And the feeling of normalcy began to slip through her fingers like water.

Jesus had grown strong and tall over the past 30 years. While Mary had seen glimpses of His divine nature, she continued to hold her breath for the day the angel prophesied would come. The words "Son of the Most High" and "His kingdom will never end" were never far from her memory. She recalled the stories of Jesus' baptism. God said, "This is my Son, whom I love; with him I am well pleased" (Matthew 3:17). Mary clung to the days of normalcy as long as she could, but she felt they were drawing to a close.

The bride was radiant and the groom proud and freshly preened. The wedding party and guests alike enjoyed a bountiful buffet, delightful dancing, and ambrosial wine. Gaiety and merriment filled the rooms with raucous laughter and prattling chatter. There was nothing like a wedding party to wash away the doldrums of everyday life.

Day three of the festivities was in full swing when Mary noticed that the wine was running low. For a groom to run out of wine was a disgrace. Mary tugged on Jesus' sleeve, and with a mischievous twinkle in her eye, she whispered, "They have no more wine."

Jesus replied, "Dear woman, why do you tell Me? My time has not come."

As soon as Jesus spoke those words, He felt the nudge from His heavenly Father: the prompting He had been waiting for His entire life. In a split second, God allowed Mary to flip the switch, to topple the first domino, to ignite the fuse. *It was time.*

Mary turned to the attendants standing nervously by the stone water jars used for ceremonial cleansing. With quiet authority, she nodded toward her son. "Do whatever He tells you to do."

Jesus pointed to six empty water jars, each with the capacity to hold 20 to 30 gallons. "Fill the jars up with water," He instructed.

Quickly, the servants dragged the heavy stone jugs to the well behind the house and filled them to the brim.

Once they had brought them back to Jesus, He continued. "Now draw some out and take it to the master of the banquet."

Continuing to follow Jesus' instructions, one of the servants dipped his ladle into the jar and poured rich, aromatic red wine into a silver goblet. He couldn't keep his eyes off the cup. Reverently the servant passed it to the master of ceremonies.

"Samuel," the master called out across the court, "you're amazing! Everyone brings out the choice wine first and then the cheaper wine after the guests have had too much to drink; but you have saved the best till now."

The servants were dumbstruck.

Jesus' friends were awestruck.

Jesus was readied.

Mary was resolved. Her time of quiet normalcy was over.

NOW'S THE TIME

And that was the beginning of Jesus' ministry of the miraculous. After 30 years of waiting, God, through Mary, gave Jesus the signal that the time for miracles had begun. Right in the middle of a pack of men—Jesus, Peter, Andrew, James, John, Philip, Nathanael, and the wine stewards—God tapped Mary on the shoulder and chose her to ignite the fuse. Let's take a closer look.

Jesus' mother said to him, "They have no more wine"
(John 2:3).

In first-century Palestine, a wedding celebration lasted for about seven days. The hosts were expected to offer proper hospitality to their guests, and that included a free-flowing supply of wine. To run out of wine was a serious offense and a social embarrassment. And here it was only three days into the festivities when Mary noticed the wine running low.

Mary saw the problem and knew just where to go to remedy the situation. But Jesus' response? "[Dear] woman, why do you involve me? My hour has not yet come" (John 2:4).

The original Greek didn't include the word *dear*. It was just *woman*. If my son called me *woman*, let's just say he wouldn't do it twice. But not so in Jesus' day. *Woman* was a polite form of address, and Jesus used it as a term of endearment.

Jesus answered His mom with, "My hour has not yet come." However, He followed through with Mary's request. Could it be that God tapped Him on the shoulder and assured Him that the time *had* indeed come? To listen to His momma? It appears so.

Do whatever he tells you (John 2:5).

These words have become my life verse. I hope they can be woven into the fabric of your own life as well. This was Mary's mantra. "May your word to me be fulfilled" became "Do whatever He tells you."

Mary isn't just speaking to the servants here. She is speaking to us as well.

Obedience to God is the key to unlocking the doors to the most exciting life imaginable, but that is no guarantee that our lives will be without pain and struggle.

Let's fast-forward three years and join Mary in one last scene.

CHOSEN TO BURY

Mary, probably now in her late forties, was startled from her mending by a pounding on the door. *Who would come here at this time of night?*

"John!" she cried as she peered through the slightly opened door. "What are you doing here? Is it Jesus?"

"Oh, Mary, I don't even know where to begin," he whispered as tears streamed down his agonized face.

"Come in, come in," Mary said as she wrapped her arm around Jesus' closest friend. "Start at the beginning."

"Well, we had a nice Passover dinner on Thursday, but I could tell that Jesus was deeply troubled. There was just something different about Him. Then He put on a towel and washed our feet! We objected and told Him we should be the ones washing His feet, but He would have none of it. And then He spoke about leaving us. Something about going to a place we didn't know. Of course, Peter said he would follow Him anywhere, even to the death. You know how Peter is."

"Yes, go on."

"After dinner we went to the Garden of Gethsemane. Jesus talked to us as we walked along the road, as if He were a father telling His sons the family secret to success before leaving to go off to war. He was so unsettled and bothered about something. When we arrived at the garden, He told us to pray for Him while He went off to be by Himself. I'm sorry to say that we fell asleep—more than once. At one point I overhead Jesus asking His Father to *let this cup pass from Him*. When I looked, Jesus had blood dripping from His brow where sweat should have been. I was going to run to Him, but before I could, an angry mob of Romans came and arrested Him!"

"Arrested Him! For what?"

"I don't know. Something about blaspheming. And guess who was at the head of the pack. Judas. I never did trust that man."

John went on to tell Mary of the trial, the flogging, and the ultimate sentencing of execution by crucifixion.

With great resolve, she looked John in the eye and said, "Take me to Him."

It seemed that all her life Mary had been trying to save Jesus. She remembered when she and Joseph fled to Egypt to escape Herod's decree to kill all the baby boys under the age of two in Bethlehem. She recalled the day she and her sons tried to convince Jesus to stop teaching the crowd and come home when she heard rumors that the Pharisees were plotting to kill Him. And now this.

Mary recalled the words of Simeon, the prophet at the temple when she and Joseph took their baby to be consecrated to the Lord: "This child is destined to cause the falling and rising of many in Israel, and to be a sign that will be spoken against, so that the thoughts of many hearts will be revealed. And a sword will pierce your own soul too" (Luke 2:34-35). This was the sword Simeon had spoken of, piercing her heart with a pain only a mother could understand.

Arriving on the Via de la Rosa, Mary watched with horror as her firstborn son trudged through the jeering crowd. His flesh hung in shreds, torn by floggings of the Roman metal-tipped whip; His body was crusted with dried blood and mud, collapsing under the weight of the cross tied to His back; and streaks of crimson cut furrows down His face from the crown of spike-like thorns pressed into His forehead.

When Jesus reached the place where His mother stood among the crowd, He raised His head to meet her gaze. A thousand thoughts passed between them without a single spoken word. She was there, just as she had been all along.

Later, as He hung on the cross, Jesus breathed His final parting words.

"Dear woman, here is your son," Jesus moaned as He nodded toward John.

And then to John He said, "Here is your mother."

Even in His last breaths, Jesus' concern was for this chosen girl from Nazareth—His mother, Mary.

RESOLVED TO REMEMBER

Mary had been there all along. She was there to hear the babe's first cry in Bethlehem and there to hear the Savior's final breath at Calvary. If we dare, let's join her at the foot of the cross and take a closer look at John's recounting of the scene.

Near the cross of Jesus stood his mother (John 19:25).

We don't have a lot of information about Mary at the foot of the cross, except that she was there—standing below her flesh-torn, blood-drenched, precious Son. She heard the hammer hit the nails, saw the Roman spear pierce His side, felt the labor of His breathing. As Jesus' heart burst, her chest ached. For six hours she watched Him die. *Pierced.* How perfectly that word described her at this moment. The sword that had hung over her head for 33 years now pierced her heart.

It must have seemed like an eternity since a symphony of angels announced His birth. Now a cacophony of accusers hurled insults and accusations. "Crucify Him!" the savage rabble demanded. "He saved others, but He can't save Himself," the chief priests and elders taunted.

Where are those angels now? she must have thought. If she could have peered into the spiritual realm, she would have seen them hovering low, silent, in full armor array.

It is sometimes difficult to envision God's presence surrounding the tragedies in our lives. Somehow the two don't seem to be able to coexist in our minds. It is almost incomprehensible to picture the angels standing by while mere humans taunted and tortured the Son of God. What do we do when life doesn't make sense? We remember God's faithfulness.

Mary remembered Gabriel's announcement.

Mary remembered Elizabeth's welcome.

Mary remembered Joseph's dreams.

Mary remembered the shepherds' arrival.

Mary remembered the magis' gifts.

Mary remembered Simeon's prophecy.

Mary remembered Anna's words.

Mary remembered the 12-year-old boy in His Father's house.

Mary remembered the water transformed to wine.

Mary remembered the miracles.

Mary remembered the teaching.

Mary remembered the healings.

Mary remembered the unborn Jesus riding on the back of a donkey the night before His birth and the Messiah Jesus riding on the back of a donkey a few days before His death.

Mary remembered.

After the shepherds' visit in the stables that first Christmas evening, Luke tells us, "Mary treasured up all these things and pondered them in her heart" (Luke 2:19). No doubt she returned to that protected trove of memories when she needed comfort and reassurance. The events of Jesus' life slipped through her mind like beads on a string with the knot of faith tied securely at the end.

And, friend, that is what we must do. The Bible tells us that in Christ "are hidden all the treasures of wisdom and knowledge" (Colossians 2:3). When we treasure God's Word in our hearts, just as Mary did in hers, it calms the waves of doubt during the storms of life. The storms may not be removed, but God's Word will help us steady the sails as we're tossed to and fro. Just as Jesus told us we have been chosen to experience the abundant life He offers (John 10:10), He also told us we will have trouble in the here and now (John 16:33). So what do we do when the waves hit? We remember the promises of God, that He will never leave us or forsake us, that He knows the beginning from the end, and that ultimately, we will rise victorious. We remember that God has a plan, and He is always working in the meanwhile to make all suffering worthwhile.

Mary knew that.

Woman, here is your son (John 19:26).

Jesus thought of Mary till the very end. Some of His last words on the cross were to her. Once again, God pulled Mary from the crowd and placed her center stage. The heavenly spotlight shone on this ordinary girl from Nazareth, and we savor her faithful resilience and obedient resolve once again.

Mary was not spared the pain and shame of having a son executed as a common criminal, but her identity did not rest on her role as a mother of a tortured son. She was less than no one. Jesus, her son and her Savior, chose to set her firmly among the disciples who would change the world.

CHOSEN TO FULFILL GOD'S PURPOSES AND HIS PLANS

Mary. Who was she? A seemingly insignificant teenage girl from an insignificant town who was chosen for the most important female role in the gospel story. She opened the door for all women to obey God with total surrender—no matter what the cost. "I am the Lord's servant. May your word to me be fulfilled" becomes our battle cry.

That type of obedience flows from a relationship of trust. It is not a burden or a "have to," but a blessing and a "get to." This is a place where our simple water is transformed into the robust wine of life. God has great plans for all of us. Paul wrote, "'What no eye has seen, what no ear has heard, and what no human mind has conceived'—the things God has prepared for those who love him" (1 Corinthians 2:9). As Mary has shown us, God sets the offer before us, but we choose whether to accept or not.

We tend to look at the Mary of Christmas and Easter, but she did a whole lot of living in between. From the cradle to the cross, God used this woman to nurture His Son, to encourage His Son, and to shore up His Son in the face of death. She began by leading her young son by the hand, and she ended with Him leading her by the heart.

God didn't *need* Mary in order for Jesus to appear on this earth. He created Adam from a little dust and spit. God *chose* for His Son to enter this world through the womb of a woman. But she was more than an incubator for the Son of God. Giving birth was not her only role. She was the first believer. The first follower. The first disciple. The first to hold Him. The first to mold Him. The first to mourn Him. She was God's chosen instrument to inaugurate Jesus' ministry as she spoke, "Do whatever He tells you."

Mary was the mother of a murdered son and the widow of a deceased husband. It would have been easy for her to fall back into insignificance at such a fate filled with brokenness. But that is not where we see her last. In her parting scene in the grand drama of her life, we see Mary with the disciples waiting for the promised Holy Spirit and her next assignment.

In the book of Acts, we meet Mary one last time. After Jesus' resurrection, He addressed the disciples before His ascent to take His seat at the right hand of the Father. He instructed them to wait for the promised Holy Spirit, reassured them that He would return again, and commissioned them to share the gospel to the ends of the earth. Then Jesus was taken up before their very eyes, and the group headed to Jerusalem to wait (Acts 1:1-14).

So who was among this commissioned group of disciples who gathered in the upper room to wait for the promised Holy Spirit? Peter, John, James, Andrew, Philip, Thomas, Bartholomew, Matthew, James, Simon, Judas son of James, the women, Mary the mother of Jesus, and His brothers. Hold everything! The women? Yes, the women. We'll find out more about those gals a bit later, but for now, note that Mary was there. For centuries the religious leaders had established an all-boys club. But now a fresh wind blew in to change the scenery of the new order called "the church." Jesus' parting words commissioned both men and women to spread the gospel.

Mary, the mother of Jesus, was among the disciples. She was a disciple, a learner, a follower. She was commissioned with the rest of the group to spread the gospel "in Jerusalem, and in all Judea and Samaria, and to the ends of the earth" (Acts 1:8). And while we don't meet up with this incredible woman again, we can be sure she did just that.

Mary was among the collective prophecies of Joel: "'In the last days, God says, I will pour out my Spirit on all people. Your sons and daughters will prophesy, your young men will see visions, your old men will dream dreams. Even on my servants, *both men and women,* I will pour out my Spirit in those days, and they will prophesy'" (Acts 2:17-18, emphasis mine; see also Joel 2:28-29).

We have to be careful not to worship Mary. Jesus didn't. When someone from a crowd yelled, "Blessed is the mother who gave you birth and nursed you," Jesus answered, "Blessed rather are those who hear the word of God and obey it" (Luke 11:27-28). Yes, God chose Mary. Yes, God chose you. He has freed us from the stigma of being less than by including women with the words: "Blessed rather are those who hear the word of God and obey it." That is where our significance lies.

Mary knew who she was. She was a chosen child of God, never less than, always more than ready to impact the world with the gospel. He called an ordinary girl center stage, and she willingly walked forward to take her place.

 Validated

A Gutsy Risk Taker

For 12 long years, she had been bleeding. More than 4,380 days. Lydia had gone from doctor to doctor to stop the flow, but as the years progressed, her condition only worsened. Each day was a reminder of the emptiness she felt as her very life ebbed from her body.

"I've lost my family, my friends, my energy, and now all my money. My womanhood—the ability to conceive a child—flows out of my body daily. And the pain? The constant cramping feels as though my womb is being squeezed by a vise, ever tightening, ever clenching.

"'Unclean.' That's what the priests say I am. No one is supposed to even touch me unless they are willing to go through a cleansing process afterward. The house I live in, the chair I sit in, the utensils I cook with—all ceremonially unclean. Oh, how I long for a human touch. A hug. A kiss. A pat on the back. A baby's cheek against my own.

"Oh, God," Lydia prayed. "There is nothing else for me to do. I've tried everything. Only a miracle will set me free from this life of isolation."

God smiled down at this daughter of Abraham. Today was the day. Sitting all alone in a darkened room, she heard a ruckus outside her window.

"It's Jesus!" someone shouted. "Jesus is coming!"

Jesus. Maybe He could heal me. I know I'm not supposed to go out in public. And I certainly cannot speak to this man or any man on the street. What can I do?

Quickly, she devised a plan. She wrapped a veil around her head and face with only her eyes peering through a slight opening. Then she snuck out of her home and merged with the throng of people trying to catch a glimpse of the much-acclaimed healer and teacher. Gathering all the courage she could muster, Lydia pushed her way through the crowd in hopes of getting close enough to touch the hem of His robe.

"Jesus!" a man called from the crowd. The multitude parted and made way for the synagogue ruler to pass. Everyone knew Jairus. He was important.

Jesus turned as Jairus fell at His feet. "My little daughter is dying," he begged. "Please come and put Your hands on her so she will be healed and live."

Lydia looked on as Jesus extended His hand to this distraught father, compassionately helping him to his feet, and apparently changing course to go with him. It was then she made her move.

Shoring up more determination than she deemed possible, Lydia began muttering to herself. "If I can but touch His clothes, I will be healed. I know it. I just know it. I can't let this opportunity slip away." While unsure of herself, she was confident in Him. Her faith overcame her fear, and she pressed forward.

Like a runner stretching for the finish line, Lydia reached through the crowd, strained toward her mark, and brushed her fingers against the hem of Jesus' garment. As soon as her fingers grazed the cloth, she felt a surge of healing course through her body. Suddenly the flow of blood stopped.

She knew it. She felt it. The flow stopped…and then Jesus stopped.

"Who just touched My robe?" He asked.

The woman kept her eyes fixed on the ground as a jumble of thoughts jostled in her mind. *I'm unclean and not supposed to be out in public. I'm not supposed to touch anyone. What am I going to do? If I remove my veil, people will recognize me.* She wanted to run, but her feet were rooted to the ground.

"Many people are crowding against You," His disciples answered. "Why do You ask, 'Who touched Me'?"

Jesus ignored His disciples and continued to scan the crowd in search of the person who had purposely touched His robe. He had felt the surge of power leave His body. He knew what had happened. Jesus could always sense the difference between the press of the curious and the purposeful reach of the seeker.

Silence hung low. No one said a word.

Finally, Lydia couldn't hold it in any longer. She turned to Jesus and fell at His feet. With a trembling voice, she confessed and told the whole story.

"Master, I have been bleeding for more than 12 years. I have gone from doctor to doctor, and no one has been able to help me. I've lost my family, my friends, and my finances. But when I heard You were passing through, I just knew that You, Lord, could heal me. I know I'm not supposed to touch anyone. I know I am unclean in all regards. Please forgive me for the intrusion. But, Jesus, what I have to tell You is this: I am healed! As soon as I touched the hem of Your robe, the blood flow stopped! Thank You, Jesus! Thank You, Jesus!"

While others began to back away from her, Jesus leaned in and blessed her. "Daughter, your faith has healed you. Go in peace and be freed from your suffering."

VALIDATED AS VALUABLE

Oh, how I love this story! What woman among us hasn't felt the wretchedness of rejection and the humility of hopelessness? What woman among us hasn't felt she was less than because of certain circumstances in her life? What woman hasn't wondered, *Would God even care about the likes of me?* And here we have a story of just how much God values and esteems His female image bearers. He singles out one lone woman from a crowd of curiosity seekers, heals her physically and spiritually, and then places her center stage to tell about it. Let's take a closer look at the story as Mark tells it.

A woman was there who had been subject to bleeding for twelve years (Mark 5:25).

The woman we meet in Mark 5 has been called "the woman with the issue of blood." She was defined by what was wrong with her. Oh, how that breaks my heart. Perhaps you've felt that way a time or two in your life. Defined by what's wrong with you, at least in your own mind. Feeling less than those around you, who feel less than others as well. We tend to compare what we know to be wrong about ourselves with what we don't know to be wrong with others. Let me just give you a hug right now and remind you, we've all got something. Resist the tendency to define yourself by what you imagine to be wrong with you, and embrace the truth of what God says is right with you. Cleansed, complete, and completely forgiven through Jesus.

As with the woman in this story and the nameless ones in the following pages, I've given this brave barrier breaker a name to help us remember that she was a flesh and blood person just like me and you. She's not just a character in a story, but a sister who struggled with life.

For 12 long years, this woman had been bleeding; we can assume it was vaginally. When we meet her, she is physically, financially, socially, and spiritually drained—bankrupt in every way.

In biblical days, certain situations and conditions rendered a person ceremonially unclean. Leprous people were separated from society and had to shout, "Unclean! Unclean!" when they walked among common folk. Anyone who touched a dead body was considered unclean. And a woman was considered unclean during her monthly cycle. What does it mean to be called "unclean"? It means the person is untouchable. Let that sink in for a moment.

For seven days, considered the time of a normal female period, a woman was secluded. A woman hemorrhaging for 12 years would be permanently quarantined. If unmarried, she would not be able to marry. If married, her condition would be grounds for divorce. She would be cut off from her family, evicted from her home, and ostracized by her community.

I'm sure each doctor's visit brought a surge of hope, only to be swept away when the red flow reappeared. The joy of tender youth was crushed by the weight of adult disappointment. The hammer of rejection drove the nails of isolation into the coffin of her broken heart.

Unlike the lame man who was lowered through the roof by four friends and placed at Jesus' feet, this woman apparently had no one to intercede for her. There was no father pleading for his daughter. There was no husband praying for his wife. There was no master imploring Jesus to help heal his servant. When we meet this woman, she is fearful and forgotten. She is all alone—or so it seemed to her.

Sometimes we can feel the same. Abandoned by friends. Deserted by a spouse. Forgotten by family. Unseen by society. But she was not forgotten. She was not alone. This daughter of Abraham was close to God's heart and foremost on His mind. So God the Father orchestrated His Son's journey to pass her way.

Resist the tendency to define your identity by what you imagine to be wrong with you and embrace God's truth that defines your identity by what Jesus did right for you.

If I just touch his clothes, I will be healed (Mark 5:28).

This woman understood that Jesus was radically different in His approach and acceptance of women. She had heard He was willing to disregard the status quo and to risk making enemies by liberating women from centuries of repression and pious tradition.

She knew full well that she was overstepping cultural and religious boundaries set out by the men of her day, but it was a risk she was willing to take.

She felt in her body that she was freed from her suffering (Mark 5:29).

Two things happened when the woman touched Jesus. First, she was healed. Then she was revealed. Her courage, cloaked in anonymity, trembled in the fear of exposure, but Jesus was not going to allow her to slip away with her healing. He wanted to do more than heal her body; He wanted to save her soul and prove to her that she was not less than anyone.

Daughter, your faith has healed you (Mark 5:34).

A rabbi did not speak to a woman in public, but once again, Rabbi Jesus broke the man-made rules for a God-made woman. He did not call her out to embarrass or shame her in any way. He wanted to honor her honesty, to commend her courage, and to validate her valor. He did not reprimand her for breaking the religious rules but praised her great faith.

Luke adds an interesting sentence in his account of this story: "Then the woman, seeing that she could not go unnoticed, came trembling and fell at his feet. *In the presence of all the people,* she told why she had touched him and how she had been instantly healed" (Luke 8:47, emphasis mine).

In the presence of all the people. Remember, this was a time in history when women were considered to be unreliable witnesses, and a woman's testimony was inadmissible and unacceptable as evidence in a court of law. But Jesus debunked their way of thinking. She was a key witness to the power of God working through His Son. There was no way He was going to let her slip away with her healing. He had work for her to do. She now had a story to tell.

Once again, Jesus called a woman from out of the shadows and placed her center stage. No longer was she a woman in need of healing, but now a healed daughter called to tell about it. He placed a woman on equal standing with men and addressed her respectfully, called her to testify unashamedly, and sent her away healthy and spiritually whole. He publicly validated her as a viable part of the community and as a child of God.

"*Daughter,* your faith has healed you." Can we just stop there for a moment? Sometimes one single word in Scripture speaks volumes. Why did Jesus call her *daughter*? It seems to me that while Jairus was concerned for his daughter, God was also concerned for His. *Daughter* was a term of endearment she would not easily forget.

When Jesus said the word *healed,* it is the Greek word *sesoken,* which means "saved." Jesus did more than heal her body. He saved her soul, removed her shame, and reestablished her place in the community. As with this particular woman and the others we will visit, Jesus viewed their needs as portals through which deeper spiritual needs might be met. His miraculous healings were the chain cutters that set women free from physical, emotional, and spiritual disease and sent them toward physical, emotional, and spiritual health. He ministered to their immediate needs and gave them an eternal perspective and great significance.

Rabbi Jesus broke the man-made
rules for a God-made woman.

THE VALUE OF A LITTLE GIRL

We can't leave this scene quite yet. If you recall, Jesus was on His way somewhere else when the woman reached out to grab hold of her healing.

> One of the synagogue leaders, named Jairus, came…"My little daughter is dying. Please come and put your hands on her so that she will be healed and live." So Jesus went with him (Mark 5:22-24).

Mingled like two skeins of yarn, the story of the bleeding woman is knit together with Jairus' dying daughter. We can't miss the time frame. The woman had suffered for 12 years. The girl had lived 12 years. The woman had a chronic illness that had lasted for years. The child had an acute sickness that sprang up overnight.

Jairus was a big shot in the local Jewish community, but the thought of losing a child made him see the truth that he was indeed very small. He might have had power in the synagogue, but he was powerless to save his little girl.

Not many religious leaders in Jesus' day openly professed a belief that Jesus was the Messiah. I've often heard the saying: "There are no atheists in foxholes." When under heavy fire and enemy attack, when the guns of adversity are blazing overhead, even the hardest heart will cry out, "God help me! God save me!"

Perhaps that is what we see in Jairus. "My little daughter is dying," he cried. "Please come and put your hands on her so that she will be healed and live."

Have you ever wondered what was going through Jairus' mind as Jesus stopped to take care of the woman who touched His robe? *Wait a minute, I was here first,* he might have thought. *My daughter is more important. Let's get this show on the road.*

Aren't you glad that Jesus has enough grace for everyone? He's not going to run out of blessings. He had enough healing power for the desperate woman and the dying girl…and enough for you and me.

Right after Jesus healed our friend with the bleeding disorder, some men came from Jairus' house and told him his daughter was dead. Jesus told the distraught father, "Don't be afraid; just believe." Jesus went to Jairus' house, cleared the little girl's room of mourners, and then took her lifeless hand in His. "Little girl, I say to you, get up!" He said. Immediately she opened her eyes, stood upon her feet, and walked around the room.

Jesus was so intentional. God was so precise. This was a culture that cared very little for women, much less young girls. But here comes Jesus, breaking cultural rules and societal norms to heal, embrace, and set God's female image bearers free. He interrupts the course of His day to attend to a languishing woman and a little girl. They were both important to Jesus. They were both important to God.

What sort of God would do that? A God who loves, cherishes, and highly esteems His grand finale of all creation—woman. This, my friend, was radical. A splash of cold water in the face of societal prejudice, discrimination, and unmitigated segregation.

THE VALUE OF THE WOMAN IN THE MIRROR

For us in the twenty-first century, it is hard to imagine bleeding from the womb for 12 years. Medical science has progressed way beyond the rudimentary knowledge of Jesus' day.

But I suggest there are still many women with chronic bleeding of a different sort. We bleed from the heart. Women wake each day with a memory that opens old wounds. Women long to hear the words, "Go in peace and be freed from your suffering."

The woman with the issue of blood was no different from you and me. While her apparent illness was physical, her inward suffering ruled her life. But in one radical moment, one momentous decision, she reached out to Jesus and grabbed hold of her healing. We are invited to do that too.

Mark used specific words to describe our friend with the issue of blood: "She had suffered a great deal" (verse 26). Jesus used the word *suffer* when He was referring to His last days on earth (Mark 8:31; 9:12). Jesus understood her suffering more than she knew. He knew about His own suffering that was to come, His own blood that would drip on the cursed ground. And He knows about yours.

Once again, Jesus took a woman who had previously moved about in the shadows of society and called her center stage. Then He validated her as a child of God. She was not less than anyone, but more than worthy to be called a daughter, co–image bearer of God, and in just a few short months, a coheir of Christ.

CHAPTER 4

Redeemed

The Rock Dropper

What are we going to do with this Jesus?" the chief priest asked the group. "He is going about healing people left and right. Everywhere I go the buzz is about Him. It's Jesus this, Jesus that. And the crowds are calling Him the Messiah! Everyone knows the Messiah will not come from Galilee. If we don't get rid of Him, we're going to have an insurrection on our hands."

"And ever since that loaves and fish situation, His followers have multiplied like the lunch he served," another priest added. "He must be stopped."

"I have an idea," Lucius responded with a gleam in his eye. "I happen to know a certain married man who is sleeping with his mistress at this very moment. I saw him slink into her house last night." And as the hard-hearted Pharisees gathered round, a mean-spirited plan to trick Jesus began to unfold.

The sun was just peeking through the securely locked shutters of Moriah's bedroom window. The early morning stillness was sweetened by birdsong on the ledge. Moriah was a tangle of sheets, arms, and legs, and the man she loved lay sleeping beside her.

"Oh, Zachariah," she whispered as her fingertips brushed a stray lock of hair from his closed eyes. "If only you could marry *me*."

Moriah's musings were interrupted by a banging on the door.

"Open up!" the gruff voice demanded.

"Who is there?" Moriah cried.

"Open up or we'll break the door down."

"What's all the commotion?" Zachariah mumbled as he groggily sat up in bed. "What's going on?"

Before Moriah could even think to answer, an angry mob of religious men broke through the simple lock and into the lovers' hideaway.

"What is the meaning of this?" Zachariah barked. "What do you think you are doing?"

"What do you think *you* are doing, my friend?" the Pharisee countered. "That is the real question here."

"Moriah, daughter of Omar, you are under arrest for adultery and breaking the law of Moses!" the moral police spat. "Get dressed and come with me."

The Pharisee tossed Moriah her night robe, but he failed to turn his head as she slipped her trembling frame from the cover of the sheets and into the thin garment. He grabbed her by the arm and began dragging her to the door.

"Where are you taking me?" she cried.

"You'll find out soon enough," the Pharisee growled.

"What about Zachariah? Isn't he guilty too?" the youngest man of the group inquired.

"Just leave him. We don't need him."

"Wait!" Zachariah called. But already he could see that protesting was no use.

"Why don't you go back to your wife?" the Pharisee called over his shoulder as the group left the room. And with that, the conspiring mob continued their trek to the temple with the half-clad, quaking woman in tow. Two men flanked her on either side, dragging her through the early morning bustle of the city. The bait was on the hook; now it was time to catch the fish.

A meddlesome stream of townsfolk joined the parade. Jesus was already teaching in the courtyard with a group gathered around Him. A distant herd of feet grew louder and louder as the curious mob and determined Pharisees approached. They marched right into the middle of the circle of listeners gathered around Jesus and thrust the woman at the Teacher's feet.

Moriah's unbound hair fell around her bare shoulders. Her shame-filled eyes stayed riveted on the ground, refusing to meet condemning eyes. Then one of the men pulled her to her feet and placed her on display.

"Teacher," the pious Pharisee began, "we caught this woman in the act of adultery. The law of Moses says she should be stoned. What do You say?"

Jesus didn't look at the woman's half-clad body. He looked into her soul.

After a moment, Moriah lifted her head and peered into the eye of love.

She heard the Pharisee's question and understood Jesus' dilemma. If He set her free, the Pharisees would accuse Him of ignoring the law of Moses and deem Him a heretic. If He sentenced her to death by stoning, His followers would question His teaching on grace and forgiveness.

The religious leaders already held stones in their clenched fists, anticipating Jesus' reply. Their hearts were as hard as the rocks in their hands. But rather than giving a quick answer, Jesus stooped to the ground and began writing in the dirt. A chill swept through the Pharisees. Beneath their robes, they felt the shame of naked exposure as Jesus looked up at each of them and silently uncloaked their sinful thoughts and desires. With one look from Jesus, they stood, their souls more exposed than the half-dressed woman before them.

Finally, Jesus rose and delivered the verdict.

"If any one of you is without sin, let him be the first to throw a stone at her."

Then He squatted once again and continued writing.

One by one the Pharisees unclenched their fists, dropped their stones, and slunk away through the crowd. The older men who had accumulated a longer list of sins turned to leave first, with the younger ones not far behind.

After the last of the Pharisees cleared the scene, Jesus straightened up and asked, "Woman, what happened to your accusers? Does no one remain to condemn you?"

"No one," she replied.

"Then neither do I condemn you," Jesus declared. "Go now and leave your sinful lifestyle once and for all."

The woman turned to leave, but not before picking up a discarded stone to take with her.

"To remember," she whispered.

FACE-TO-FACE WITH GRACE

Jesus' ministry and miracles caused quite a stir everywhere He put His sandaled feet. His authoritative teaching to the masses, passionate clearing out of the temple courts, and confusing prophecy of the destruction and resurrection of the temple made people sit up and take notice. Jesus expanded His ministry to include the shunned Samaritans and Syrophoenician Gentiles. He commanded a lame man to take up his pallet and walk, and He fed 5,000 men—plus women and children—with no more than five loaves and two fish. The multitudes wanted to make Jesus king. The scribes and Pharisees wanted to make Jesus disappear.

Jesus knew the Jewish religious leaders wanted to kill Him, yet He continued ministering publicly and prophetically. They looked for reasons to discredit and denounce Him, so they came up with a plan to publicly humiliate Him by putting Him in what they thought was a no-win situation. Let's take a closer look at how they used a woman as bait but were snared by their own trap.

Jesus went to the Mount of Olives (John 8:1).

The night before this incident, Jesus had been on the Mount of Olives praying. The mount is directly east of Jerusalem and rises about 2,700 feet. This summit offered a magnificent view of the city and the temple below. How appropriate that Jesus would spend His time alone with God looking down at the apple of His eye.

He sat down to teach (John 8:2).

Early the next morning, Jesus came to the temple to teach. John tells us "all the people gathered around." When I see the word *all*, I think *all*. The radical Rabbi was teaching both men and women. And even though the present culture did not even count women as people, as we see in the recording of Jesus feeding 5,000 men who were counted and a multitude of women who were not, Jesus taught in places where women would naturally gather.

Teacher, this woman was caught in the act of adultery (John 8:4).

The Sanhedrin, or religious leaders, forced their way into the center of those gathered around Jesus and interrupted His teaching. I suspect Jesus was expecting them all along.

The fact that she was "caught in the act" smells of a setup. Perhaps they planned the tryst and planted a man to seduce her. Or the relationship could have been common knowledge, and everyone had turned a blind eye until this opportunity to exploit it. There were no video cameras or private investigators with revealing photos back then, so when they say, "caught in the act," that means they walked in on the scene. Whatever the case, they knew where to find her and what she would be doing.

I doubt these men gave the accused time to fully clothe herself or pin her hair back in place. The idea of a woman walking through the streets with her hair unbound was scandalous enough, much less being half dressed and manhandled by angry pious priests.

The Pharisees were considered the "custodians of public morality."[1] They were supposed to be the good guys, but in most biblical accounts they were the bad guys. Jesus said this about the religious leaders: "You study the Scriptures diligently because you think that in them you have eternal life. These are the very Scriptures that testify about me, yet you refuse to come to me to have life" (John 5:39-40).

These men had the Scriptures in their heads and were pretty proud about that. But they didn't have God in their hearts and were pretty blind about that.

There was no denying the accusation. So they cast the bait.

In the Law Moses commanded us to stone such women. Now what do you say? (John 8:5).

Ah, excuse me, boys, but someone is missing here. Last time I checked, it takes two to commit adultery. As for the law, let's take a look at what it really said:

> If a man commits adultery with another man's wife—with the wife of his neighbor—both the adulterer and the adulteress are to be put to death (Leviticus 20:10).

If a man is found sleeping with another man's wife, both the man who slept with her and the woman must die. You must purge the evil from Israel (Deuteronomy 22:22).

It seems they were baiting the hook with only half a worm.

While we do not know if this woman was another man's wife, it was not the first time, and would not be the last, that a woman was left alone to carry the consequences of sexual sin. Jesus didn't address this detail, most likely because He knew that seeking justice was not the purpose of the Pharisees' visit in the first place. They couldn't have cared less about the morality issue or the law of Moses. If they were truly interested in keeping the law, then both partners would have been standing before Him. Their only concern was setting a trap.

To those looking on, it might appear that Jesus was caught between a rock and a hard place. But they didn't realize that since Jesus *is* the Rock, there is no hard place He can't handle.

Jesus bent down and started to write on the ground with his finger (John 8:6).

I'm sure it threw them off a bit when Jesus stooped to write in the dirt. This is the only time that Scripture records Jesus writing anything. Could it be that He was trying to distract the people's attention away from the half-dressed woman and onto Himself? It sounds just like something my Jesus would do.

What did Jesus write? Nobody knows for sure. Some commentaries suggest He scribbled down the sins of the Pharisees. Some suggest He was doodling to present a pregnant pause or give the accusers time to think. What He wrote is not important, but what He said was powerful.

Let any one of you who is without sin be the first to throw a stone at her (John 8:7).

What an answer! Jesus uncovered their own hearts and left them exposed and spiritually naked before the crowd. Now who was stuck between a rock and a hard place? Each man standing knew his own life was riddled with sin. The prophet Isaiah, whose writings they knew very well, wrote: "We all, like sheep, have gone astray, each of us has turned to our own way" (Isaiah 53:6). For a man to throw a stone and thus imply that he was without sin would have been the greatest heresy of all.

Isn't it interesting that the only person qualified to throw a stone at the woman is the One who set her free?

Again he stooped down and wrote on the ground
(John 8:8).

Sometimes the shortest answers are the most powerful. Jesus gave His answer and then let them think on it. No hurry. Just chew on that for a while. I think it would be a good time for us to chew on it ourselves. If I were sitting right there with you, I'd want us to chat about what "Let any one who is without sin throw the first stone" means in our own lives. It is easy to smirk at those self-righteous, pious Pharisees and say, "Ha! Take that!" But what about you and me? When is the last time you or I threw a stone at someone? Maybe not a literal stone, but a stone-hard judgmental attitude tossed someone's way? Even the smallest stone is too heavy for us to carry.

Those who heard began to go away one at a time, the
older ones first (John 8:9).

The Pharisees brought the woman to be condemned, but Jesus freed her by extending grace. The accusers came to Jesus in self-righteous superiority, but they skulked away in self-defeated shame. The accusers became the accused.

Many commentaries note that Jesus and the woman were left alone. However, before the confrontation began, Jesus was teaching "all" who came to the temple to hear Him. There is no indication that those people left. It could be that only the accusers slipped away. I imagine the onlookers were glued to their seats watching the drama unfold. I know I would have been.

But as Jesus so often does, He sees through the crowd and zooms in on one hurting soul that needs His attention. One woman who felt less than because of her past mistakes and failures.

Has no one condemned you? (John 8:10).

The Pharisees spoke accusatorily about her. Jesus spoke respectfully to her. The woman caught in adultery stood before Jesus in disgrace but was met with divine grace. That's my Jesus. We do not read of this woman's verbal statement of faith, but Jesus knew what was in her heart. He knew she was repentant, and He freed her *from* condemnation and freed her *to* start anew. The religious leaders put her down like dirt. Jesus looked at her with compassion and lifted her out of it. How refreshing it must have been to meet a man who was not interested in exploiting her but freeing her.

LIVING IN YOUR GRACE SPACE

Maybe you haven't been caught in the act of adultery. Maybe you have. But we all have pages of our stories that we'd like to rip out, sentences we'd like to block out, and chapters we'd like to throw out. Know this, sister: The splinter of your story that you hate the most does not define the entire narrative. You are more than your worst pages. Why? Because of grace.

Friend, you are never less than because of your past mistakes and failures. When you ask God to forgive you, He does. John wrote, "If we confess our sins, he is faithful and just and will forgive us our sins and purify us from all unrighteousness" (1 John 1:9).

Notice Jesus said to the woman, "Go now and leave your life of sin" (John 8:11). That is the very definition of repentance—to turn and go in the opposite direction. Let's be very clear. Jesus did not say that what the woman did was okay. He called sin a sin. And yet He extended grace and opened the door for her to start anew—to write a new chapter to her story. And that's exactly what He does for me and you.

In another book I wrote, "We can wrest redemption from the jaws of brokenness and then allow God to use it for good."[2] Shame is a universal destroyer of destinies, dignity, and callings, and when Jesus says, "Then neither do I condemn you; go and sin no more," we must believe Him and take Him up on the offer. To refuse is to continue in a story line that will bring nothing but heartache.

Your greatest mistakes have the potential to become your greatest miracles. This encounter with Jesus as He extended grace rather than throwing a rock was her miracle. Our encounter with Jesus' grace is ours.

Friend, you are never less than because
of your past mistakes and failures.

CHAPTER 5

Pursued

The Empty Bucket

The harsh midday sun beat down through a cloudless sky, and the morning breeze had long since stilled. The weary, worn woman picked up her empty jug and her empty life and headed to Jacob's well to draw her daily supply of water.

Jacob's well was a bustling place for community life among the women in the small village. It was their one chance to leave the confines of home and mingle with friends. They caught up on the latest gossip, exchanged village news, and shared homemaking tips. Most women came to the well in groups. But Ramona ventured out alone.

"It would be nice if I could go to the well in the cool of the morning or the calm of the evening like all the other women," she mumbled to herself. "But it's just not worth it. I'm tired of the condescending stares. Why, last week, Sarah yanked her five-year-old daughter's arm to keep her from getting too close to me. Did she think I would contaminate her if she brushed my robe?" Ramona peeked out of the door. High noon. The coast was clear.

The Samaritan woman balanced the five-gallon water jug atop her veiled head and made her way to the community well. Her thoughts of rejection continued as she plodded down the dusty trail. *All I've ever longed for was to be wanted and loved. What's so wrong with that? Five times I've tried and five times I've been rejected. Married and divorced, married and divorced. Tossed away like an old sandal.*

Ramona's thoughts were interrupted as she reached her destination and noticed a lone man sitting by the well's edge. *What's a Jew doing in a place like this? I'll just keep my eyes down and pretend He isn't there.*

But He *was* there. And He was there for a reason.

His unexpected words startled her.

"Could I bother you for a drink?" He asked.

A Jewish man would never stoop so low as to speak to a Samaritan woman, she thought. *He's just like all other men. He won't speak to me in public where people can see but is all too eager to engage when he wants something. I'll show him.* With a hint of sarcasm, the woman replied, "I'm a bit confused. You are a Jew and I am a Samaritan, and yet you ask me for a drink. Isn't that against the rules?"

Jesus ignored her sarcasm and cut right to the chase. He was more interested in winning the woman than winning the war of words. "If you only knew who I am, you would be asking Me for a drink, and I would give you living water."

Now He had her attention. What in the world was living water? Who was this man? Without realizing it, she lowered her water jug and began lowering her emotional walls as well.

"And how are you going to get this living water?" she laughed. "You don't even have a bucket. Are you just going to reach down into the well with your hands? Our forefather, Jacob, gave us this well. Are you saying you are greater than Jacob? That you can give us something better than he has given?" Even though Jesus was trying to move her thinking from a physical need to spiritual truth, she was not quick to follow.

"Drink from this well," Jesus continued, "and you'll be thirsty again.

But if you drink from the well that I'm speaking of, the well of living water, your thirst will be quenched forever. Not only that, but you'll also have a spring of water living inside you that will bubble up and spill over onto those around you."

"Give me that water!" she said. "Oh, how I'd love to never come to this well again!"

The woman didn't understand what "living water" was all about, but if it meant she didn't have to come to the well every day and face the condemning comments and stony stares from the other women in the town, she wanted it.

"Go, get your husband and come back."

Suddenly, shame hit Ramona hard. All those feelings of being unwanted weighed heavy upon her heart.

"I don't have a husband," she flatly replied, retreating behind a face used to hiding her emotions.

"You are right," Jesus continued. "I'm glad you admitted it. I applaud your honesty. The truth is, you have had five husbands and the man you're living with right now is not your husband. So you are telling the truth when you say you don't have a husband."

There was not a hint of condemnation in Jesus' voice. He simply stated the facts as though He was noting the day's weather or the price of eggs at the market.

How does this stranger know about me? Who is this man? Is he a prophet?

Trying to skirt the real issue, the woman tried to engage Jesus in a theological debate and veer the discussion away from her sorry life. "Sir, I get the idea that you are a prophet. Our fathers worshipped on this mountain, but you Jews claim that the place where we must worship is in Jerusalem. Which is it?"

"Believe Me," Jesus said. "One day you will worship the Father neither on this mountain nor in Jerusalem. A time is coming and actually has now come, when the true worshippers will worship the Father in spirit and truth. That's what God really wants. It is not about where you worship, but who and how."

"Oh, well," she shrugged, "I know the Messiah is coming. When He comes, He will explain everything to us."

Jesus looked intently into the woman's eyes, and for the first time in His ministry, He told someone His true identity. "I am He."

In her heart, she knew it was true. She wouldn't have been able to explain how she knew, but she knew. The woman wanted to laugh, to cry, to worship at His feet, but before she could do any of those things, a cloud of dust and the rumble of male voices interrupted their conversation. Jesus' friends had returned from the market and stopped short, amazed that He was talking to a woman—a Samaritan woman. But even more startling than who He was talking to was what He had said: "I am He."

Leaving her water pot, the woman ran back to town and told the townsfolk about the Messiah she met at Jacob's well.

WAITING BY THE WELL

I have to tell you, this is one of my favorite passages in the Bible. It is filled with hope for any woman who has ever felt abused, misused, or forgotten. It holds great promise for any woman who has ever tried to fill the hole in her heart with relationships but come up empty. It is for every single one of us who has ever felt less than because we were tossed away or others were chosen and we were not.

This passage is the longest recorded conversation between Jesus and any one single person in the entire New Testament…and it is with a woman. That in itself is radical! It was also intentional. Let's take a seat by the edge of the well and eavesdrop a little as John tells the story.

He left Judea and went back once more to Galilee (John 4:3).

Jesus had been very busy in Judea and was on His way back to Galilee. It wasn't persecution that drove Him away, but incredible success.

His increasing popularity caused Him to retreat as the Pharisees began to see Him as a threat.

The shortest route from Judea to Galilee lay on a high road straight through Samarian territory, but the Jews routinely crossed the Jordan River and took the long way around to avoid going through the towns of the despised Samaritans. In 721 BC, the Assyrians conquered Israel and deported thousands of Israelites to the land between Mount Gerizim and Ebal. There the Israelites intermarried with foreigners and became known as Samaritans.

Jews avoided Samaritans like the plague—literally. They were quarantined, and the Jews kept their distance. And the Samaritans hated the Jews right back.

So it wasn't because of geography that Jesus "had to go through Samaria." Oh, no. He "had to go through Samaria" because His Father told Him to. Jesus reminded the disciples many times that He only did what His Father told Him to do, so we know Jesus was there on special assignment. It was not a coincidence or a casual meeting, but a "deliberate, intentional, and calculated decision on the part of the Savior of the world to go meet with her."[1] You see, there was a woman in Samaria who had been used and abused all her life. She felt less than every man who had thrown her away, as well as every woman who looked the other way. And now she was about to experience something new: being pursued by pure love.

The longest recorded conversation between Jesus and any one single person in the entire New Testament was with a woman.

It feels almost outrageous to think of God pursuing me. He is God. I am but dust. And yet God does pursue *me*. He does pursue *you*. I am undone trying to grasp an inkling of the incomprehensible possibility and the absurdity of it all. Shouldn't I be the one pursuing God? Isn't that what I've done all my life? Isn't that what theologians wrote about for centuries? And yet, everywhere I look, I catch glimpses of God pursuing me—romancing me. That's what we see Him doing with the woman by the well.

While she may have felt less than all the other townswomen with seemingly more pristine reputations, she was the woman God handpicked to become the first evangelist to Samaria. Oh yes, she may have been five times rejected by man, but she was for all time chosen by God. And amazingly, God sent His Son to offer her a personal invitation.

So Jesus had to go. Not because of geography, but because of a master plan. As it is with our own lives, we may not see God's strategic maneuvering, but we must believe that He is always working behind the scenes. While it may appear that everything is falling apart, it could be that the pieces are actually falling into place. And while the disciples went shopping for groceries, Jesus waited patiently for His assignment to show up.

It was about noon (John 4:6).

By Jewish time it was the sixth hour—the heat of the day. While most women went to the well to draw water for their daily use in the cool of the morning or late in the evening, this woman went at high noon to avoid being snubbed by the other women in town. She preferred the heat of the sun to the cold shoulders of the women. So while the women gathered with their friends to catch up on the latest gossip, the one they gossiped about stayed away. She waited until the others returned to their safe havens in order to find safety of her own.

Will you give me a drink? (John 4:7).

It's interesting that Jesus waited until the disciples were off doing an errand. I don't think for a minute that was by accident. Jesus planned to have a private personal conversation with this chosen woman.

Notice Jesus didn't demand a drink of water. He never does. He simply asked. This may not seem all that strange to us, but remember, Jewish men didn't talk to women in public. Jewish men didn't talk to Samaritans, period. And for a Jewish man to drink from a Samaritan woman's cup was mind-blowingly radical. He would be deemed unclean by the religious rule makers. This was scandalous. Once again, Jesus broke the man-made rules to pursue the God-made woman. He spoke to her directly and respectfully. There is no doubt Jesus' attitude and actions were shockingly different from those of any other Jewish man she had ever met before.

If you knew the gift of God (John 4:10).

What happens when someone says to you, "If you only knew"? I don't know about you, but it makes me *want to know*. Jesus' "If you only knew" made her even thirstier than she was before she came to the well. Jesus was engaging her in conversation. Inviting her to know more. Pursuing her heart.

The well was more than a hundred feet deep, but God's love was deeper still. While she was focused on drawing physical water, Jesus continued drawing her closer to living water. The water in Jacob's well would alleviate physical thirst temporarily. The water in Jesus' well would quench spiritual thirst eternally.

Helen Keller was deaf, blind, and mute. Her tutor and caregiver, Annie Sullivan, tried and tried to teach Helen sign language by associating various words with signs she made in the girl's palm. One day, as refreshing water from an outside pump ran over Helen's hands, she realized that the cold fluid flowing over her body was the symbol that Annie made in her hand. *W-a-t-e-r.* "I knew then that 'w-a-t-e-r' meant the wonderful cool something that was flowing over my hand," Helen said. "That living word awakened my soul, gave it light, joy, set it free!"[2] Thus began Helen's journey of one of her most incredible discoveries—words.

When we understand the concept of living water, it has that same effect. God "awakens our soul, gives us light, joy, sets us free!" But our woman at the well wasn't quite there yet.

Sir, give me this water so that I won't get thirsty (John 4:15).

Wait a minute. Did she say, "Give me that water"? Isn't that what Jesus asked from her? As Jesus often does, He asked her to give Him something, only to offer something better in return. That is the very definition of redemption.

The man you now have is not your husband (John 4:18).

Jesus lifted the curtain for the first big reveal—the sad truth of her life. Five husbands plus one extra. We don't know why she had been divorced five times. In those days, a man could divorce his wife if she went outside the home with her hair unbound or spoke to a man in public. He could even divorce her if she burned the bread or if he just didn't like her anymore. It didn't take much. But whatever the reasons, this was a woman who had been abused, misused, and tossed away by men she had trusted and loved.

This also gives us a hint that she was not a young woman. It takes time to experience that much rejection. No doubt the years of heartache and broken dreams were etched on her sun-scorched face. Like the rising bucket full of hope from the well of each new marriage, her dreams spilled out on the parched grounds of divorce—five times. Her longing for love left her empty and led her to yet another poor decision—man number six.

Notice that Jesus spoke to her of her past without a hint of condemnation or rejection in His voice. As a matter of fact, He applauded her honesty.

Jesus always moves the conversation to a personal level when He is about to set someone free. And He was rattling the prison keys. But she would have none of it. Quickly, she tried to change the subject.

"Sir," the woman said, "I can see that you are a prophet. Our ancestors worshiped on this mountain, but you Jews claim that the place where we must worship is in Jerusalem" (John 4:19-20).

What do we do when confronted with such naked truth about ourselves? Oftentimes we try to divert the discussion. That's exactly what this woman did. She wanted to get the spotlight off of her and onto some theological debate. *"Let's not talk about me,"* she seemed to say. *"Let's talk about religion instead."*

Jesus always brings the subject back to me—and to you. That's what is important to Him. Jesus answered her question by explaining that God is more interested in how we worship than where we worship. He is more concerned with a personal relationship than our religious practices.

Interestingly, first she called Jesus "a Jew." Then she called Him "sir." And now, confronted with the reality of her life, she calls Him "a prophet." But there was one more name she was yet to discover. A second big reveal.

I, the one speaking to you—I am he (John 4:26).

In the Greek, the original language of the New Testament, the word *he* is not used in verse 26. Literally, Jesus said, "I who speak to you am."[3] This goes back to the book of Exodus, when Moses said to God,

> "Suppose I go to the Israelites and say to them, 'The God of your fathers has sent me to you,' and they ask me, 'What is his name?' Then what shall I tell them?" God said to Moses, "I AM WHO I AM. This is what you are to say to the Israelites: 'I AM has sent me to you'" (Exodus 3:13-14).

God said His name is I AM. YHWH. When Jesus said, "I am" in John 4:26, He was equating Himself with God. Later, in John 8:58, He said, "Very truly I tell you...before Abraham was born, I am!" He was expressing His eternal existence and complete oneness with God.

Never before had Jesus come right out and told someone that He was the Messiah. Never again, until the day of His trial, would He repeat those words. And yet this abused and misused Samaritan woman who had been rejected by man was chosen by God to hear it first.

His disciples returned and were surprised to find him talking with a woman (John 4:27).

Can you imagine? The disciples came back from their grocery shopping to find Jesus talking to not just any woman, mind you, but a *Samaritan* woman. He was breaking all the rules…again. Jesus risked His reputation to save hers. I'm sure the disciples were shocked at what Jesus said and whom He said it to. The Bible says they were "surprised." But because they respected Him, they kept quiet.

No doubt, these 12 men thought they were extra special. I mean, who wouldn't? They were some of Jesus' best friends—the chosen ones. But Jesus always seemed to have a way of putting them in their place. "The first shall be last." "Serve like Me." "Wash each other's feet." So here they came upon the scene of Jesus speaking with a Samaritan woman and using her as a visual aid to teach them. That, my friend, would have been humbling. "You boys want to see how it's done? Watch this."

God's timing of the day's events was no coincidence. If they had arrived earlier, they would have interrupted the conversation. If they had arrived later, they would have missed Jesus' big reveal. As God would have it, they arrived just in time to hear Jesus say, "I who speak to you am He." She heard it. They heard it. The timing of their absence and subsequent arrival points once again to God's divine control over time and events.

By now, the disciples had probably figured out that Jesus had His own way of doing things. But they were slow, oh so slow, to understand that part of Jesus' plan was to liberate women from the cultural, societal, and religious shackles that had them bound.

Jesus' plan was to liberate women
from the cultural, societal, and religious
shackles that had them bound.

Could this be the Messiah? (John 4:29).

Do you think Jesus knew where the woman was going and what she was going to do? Of course He did. And He didn't try to stop her. He didn't say, "Hold up, little sister. This is just between you and Me. You can't be going out there like some kind of evangelist. Women don't do that. Nobody's going to listen to you. Just leave that job to the boys. We'll take it from here."

No. Probably with a smile on His face, Jesus watched as she excitedly left her water pot by the well and sprinted back to town with the news. *Look at her go,* He must have mused. I think He probably laughed.

Then Jesus turned to the stunned disciples. He knew what they were thinking. But rather than address their judgmental questions, He explained what was about to happen: The fields were ripe for harvest, and the reaper had gone to gather the crop for eternal life. Then He turned their attention to a newly appointed member of the workforce as she—a woman—gathered in this particular crop. She collected low-hanging fruit ripe for the picking and shuttled the harvest to the Master awaiting their arrival. In effect, Jesus was saying, "Take note, boys. Pay attention. This little lady will show you how it's done." Just as He finished His lesson on sowing and reaping, the woman returned with the entire village in tow. Jesus used her actions as a teaching tool for His closest friends.

He told me everything I ever did (John 4:39).

The people didn't come to Jesus because the woman entered into a theological debate with them. They came to Jesus because of her testimony. Revelation 12:11 says the believers overcame Satan "by the blood of the Lamb and by the word of their testimony." Isn't it amazing that our words, the words of what Jesus has done in our lives, have enough power to even be in the same sentence with "the blood of the Lamb"? And boy, did she have a story to tell.

This woman's life had been no fairytale, but it did have a fairytale ending. Her Prince had come.

PURSUED TO PURSUE

We don't know her name, but Jesus did. Not only that: He knew everything about her. He knows our names, our dreams, and our secret sins as well. Jesus knows our past, present, and future mistakes. And yet He chooses us for specific purposes in His kingdom work. Nothing will stand in His way of using whomever He chooses—not even our own messy lives.

And even though women in those days were not considered credible witnesses in a court of law, this woman was the witness God chose to spread the good news of Jesus Christ to an entire town. She left her water jug, symbolic of her old parched life, and ran to splash the news of the Messiah's arrival on anyone who would listen. And they believed her! It's hard to ignore a changed life. It might have been the first time God used a woman to evangelize a community, but it sure wouldn't be the last.

General William Booth, the founder of the Salvation Army, is said to have mused, "Some of my best men are women!" In the nineteenth century, the women of the Salvation Army went through the slums of England working where the police were afraid to venture. Neighborhoods were ruled by criminals, and the streets were a breeding ground for violence and every sort of evil. But the women of the Salvation Army bravely marched onto this battleground. William's wife, Catherine, was a well-known preacher at the time. William never held her back but encouraged her to use the gifts God had given her. I can see Jesus smiling at Catherine in the dark streets of England and thinking, *Look at her go.*

In the early 1800s, John and Charles Wesley led a period of great spiritual awakening in England and America. Their mother, Susanna, preached to more than 200 people every week in prayer meetings, which she led in her husband's parish. Later, John used women leaders for small groups called "classes," which fueled the revival.

And how thankful I am to Dr. Henrietta Mears of Hollywood's First Presbyterian Church in Los Angeles, who led a Bible study which a young man named Bill Bright attended. Under her teaching, Bright gave his life to Christ. He later went on to establish Campus Crusade for Christ (now known as Cru), an organization that has helped lead an estimated 54.5 million people to Jesus. Bill Bright's booklet *The Four Spiritual Laws* has been distributed to over 100 million people since 1952. The ministry's video, *The Jesus Film Project*, has led 490 million people to make decisions for Christ. And it all started in Henrietta Mears's Bible study.

Before his death, Billy Graham, who was also mentored by Henrietta Mears, had this to say:

> I have known Dr. Henrietta Mears for approximately fifteen years. She has had a remarkable influence, both directly and indirectly on my life. In fact, I doubt if any other woman outside of my wife and my mother has had such a marked influence. Her gracious spirit, her devotional life, her steadfastness for the simple gospel, and her knowledge of the Bible have been a continual inspiration and amazement to me. She is certainly one of the greatest Christians I have ever known.[4]

Henrietta Mears never married or bore children of her own, but she had great significance in the kingdom of God. She threw herself into God's purposes for her generation, and what a crop she produced!

I'll never forget when I spoke at a retreat in Massachusetts. About 300 women had gathered in a hotel for a weekend of praise and worship, prayer and teaching. We opened our Bibles together, joined hands in prayer, and blended voices in praise. Among the 300 women, in a far corner of the room, sat one man who ran the sound system. From the very beginning session on Friday night, God pricked my heart to pray for George.

Sunday morning, we all stood and praised God for His amazing transforming work among the women over the past 48 hours. We especially thanked God for our new brother in Christ—George the sound man. Because earlier that morning, George had accepted Jesus as his Savior. I had no idea George was even listening throughout the weekend, but God did. And George came to the altar not because of the words of just one woman, but several.

Imagine that. God used women, an army of evangelists, to enlist God's latest recruit. The Psalmist wrote, "The Lord announces the word, and the women who proclaim it are a mighty throng" (Psalm 68:11).

Our friend at the well had been a social outcast, but Jesus cast His net and drew her in. He replaced her feelings of rejection with a sense of respect, and He used her as the catalyst for the salvation of many.

The disciples went into town because they were hungry. The woman went into town to get hungry people. She was no longer a second-class citizen relegated to the back row of the balcony; now she had a front-row seat to the greatest show on earth. And at just the right moment, Jesus pulled her from the crowd and placed her center stage to play a leading role.

Why did John include this story in his Gospel? As he wrote at the end of his book, "These are written that you may believe that Jesus is the Messiah, the Son of God, and that by believing you may have life in his name" (John 20:31). I think God made sure this story was included for every woman who has ever felt less than because of rejection, discrimination, or a sullied reputation. And for you…and for me. God's pursuit began in the Garden of Eden with the words, "Where are you?" and continued with the words "Jesus had to go to Samaria." Listen closely. They continue even now.

CHAPTER 6

Accepted

The Party Crasher

H ave you heard?" the vendor at the marketplace whispered. "Jesus is in town, and He is having dinner at Simon's house!"

Upon hearing the news, Bethany's heart quickened as she remembered the first time she saw Jesus.

She had been among the crowd at the temple court when the religious leaders interrupted Jesus' teaching and dragged a half-dressed woman caught in the act of adultery before them. The Pharisees displayed the woman like a prize catch, and baited Jesus about how she should be punished. He said, "Let any one who is without sin throw the first stone."

One by one the men dropped their stones and walked away. Bethany moved closer to the front so she wouldn't miss what Jesus would say to the accused.

"Neither do I condemn you. Go and leave your life of sin."

Bethany felt as if Jesus had spoken directly to her, even though she hid behind her veil among the crowd. Then Jesus turned as if He knew exactly where she was standing and looked straight at her. Without a word, it was as if He said, "This grace is extended to you, too, My friend."

The buzz around town was: "Who is this who forgives sins?" And Bethany knew. In her heart she knew that this was the promised Messiah, the One of whom Isaiah spoke. Hadn't Jesus even quoted the prophet?

> The Spirit of the Sovereign LORD is on me, because the LORD has anointed me to proclaim good news to the poor. He has sent me bind up the brokenhearted, to proclaim freedom for the captives and release from darkness for the prisoners, to proclaim the year of the LORD's favor (Isaiah 61:1-2).

Isaiah had described her perfectly: poor, brokenhearted, captive, prisoner, mournful, grieving, and despairing. *If Jesus could forgive the woman caught in adultery, perhaps He could forgive me as well,* she hoped.

Oh, how she longed to be free of her past. Free of the shame and condemnation that followed her sinful and promiscuous lifestyle. Free from the shunning silence and loathing looks of the village women. Free from the abuse and misuse of her body among the men willing to pay for a few moments of pleasure. Free from the sickness of her soul.

Now, hearing that He was in town, she was compelled to run to Him and worship the One who could set her free.

"I must go to Him," she whispered, "but I can't go empty-handed. What gift could I take this holy man?"

Her gaze settled on the alabaster jar resting on the roughly hewn mantel. Her ability to show true love had been sealed shut like the ointment in this fragile container. Cold. Hard. Impermeable.

She held the fine Egyptian marble in her hand. The delicately carved cream-colored vial contained pure nard, an undiluted costly perfume. The feathery veins of the stone reminded her of the twisted and convoluted roads of her life, and the cold, hard stone mirrored the impenetrable walls of her heart. But then she remembered how one look from Jesus penetrated those protective walls.

"'Then neither do I condemn you.' That's what He said," she whispered.

Though small enough to fit in the palm of her hand, the vial's fragrant content was strong enough to permeate a room. It was her only valuable possession. *What can I give Him?* she asked herself. *I'll give Him all I have.*

The woman pushed through the crowds on the dusty streets of Capernaum. "Have you seen Him? Have you seen Jesus?" she asked. "I heard He was in town. Do you know where He is?"

"Yes," someone sneered. "But what would He want with the likes of you?"

"Where is He?" she begged. "Please tell me. Where is He?"

"He's having dinner at Simon the Pharisee's house, but you'll not be welcomed there. Women aren't allowed inside."

Ignoring the warning, she picked up the corners of her robe, clutched the small jar to her breast, and ran to the house of the Pharisee. Bethany burst through the wooden doors and scanned the room for Jesus.

"You can't go in there," someone called. "You'll have to stand out here like the rest of us to pick up any scraps that are left behind."

They didn't understand. She was not coming for food. She was coming to receive forgiveness.

Then she saw Him. There He was. Reclining at the crowded table on His left side with His feet tucked behind His right. The dinner guests disappeared from Bethany's focus as she walked slowly and intentionally toward Jesus. The men began to turn from their conversations and follow her across the room with their eyes. Some knew her by reputation; some because they had been paying customers.

Slowly, ignoring the condescending stares of the all-male dinner guests, she gingerly knelt beside Jesus and cupped His feet in her hands. His precious feet. Tears pooled in her eyes, years of pent-up anguish spilling over. In an intimate act reserved only for a husband, Bethany pulled the pins from her raven hair and let it cascade over her shoulders. Then she took the strands and gently wiped Jesus' feet, kissing them as she wept.

A hush filled the room. All eyes were fixed on this woman kneeling at Jesus' feet—and at Jesus allowing her to do so. All eyes. All male eyes.

Still weeping, the woman pulled the alabaster jar from the folds of her robe, broke its neck, and poured the perfumed oil on Jesus' feet. When the jar broke, she became whole. The perfume she had once doled out to lure men for a night of sinful pleasure she now emptied out on the One who gave her eternal life. The fragrance of grace circled the room and clung to the unsuspecting crowd.

After a brief conversation with Simon, Jesus placed His hand on Bethany's head and gently spoke. "Your sins are forgiven. Your faith has saved you; go in peace."

POURED OUT PRAISE

Who was this woman? Why did she cross the gender boundaries and brave the condemning crowd to see Jesus? What was the significance of the perfume? What can we learn from her courageous act? Let's take a closer look at how Luke described the scene.

He went to the Pharisee's house (Luke 7:36).

Simon was a Pharisee—a religious leader. The name *Pharisee* actually means "separated or pious one." As teachers of the law, they separated themselves from the unrighteous or unclean. They set up strict boundaries between holy and ordinary people. They did not allow unrighteous people to touch them. Of course, they were the ones who defined who was and was not righteous, which was not right at all. As I mentioned before, they were often called the bruised and bleeding ones because when they saw a woman, they would close their eyes and bump into objects. (Excuse me here, but that served them right!)

But as we know, our sweet Jesus disregarded man-made boundaries and stepped right into human hearts. He was no ordinary man, but He came to save ordinary people like you and me. From the shepherds on the hillside who were the first to hear the good news of His birth to the woman at the well drawing her daily supply of water—they were ordinary people all.

But on this occasion, Jesus was having dinner with the very group of people who would soon put Him to death.

She began to wet his feet with her tears (Luke 4:38).

Here we have yet another woman with no name. I have called her Bethany just to help us remember that she was an actual, real-life woman, not just a character in a story. I am particularly drawn to these nameless gals because we can fill in the blanks with our own names. She was referred to as "the sinful woman," "the woman who anointed Jesus," and "the woman with the alabaster jar." The Amplified Bible calls her a "notorious" sinner, and a social "outcast, devoted to sin." The New Living Translation describes her as "a certain immoral woman" (verse 37).

The truth is, Luke doesn't say she was a prostitute. Scholars have assumed she was, but what she did for a living is not really the point. She could have been a thief or even a gossip. Let's just see her as Luke intended: as a sinful woman. That, we can all relate to.

Now, can you see yourself walking into a room full of gawking men? Can you taste salty tears? Can you smell the sweat of first-century unbathed men? Can you hear the whispers of judgment? Can you feel the pounding heart in your chest?

We don't know exactly where this particular woman first met

Jesus. It could have been at the temple when the Pharisees brought the woman caught in adultery. It could have been at any number of His teaching sites or His miraculous healings. We don't know where or when, but we do know that at some point she had encountered or at least heard of His forgiving grace.

And let's not forget the specifics of her intrusion. Women were not allowed to eat with the men. They were not even allowed to serve at gatherings such as this one. It was a boys-only event all the way around. And yet this courageous woman stepped right across the forbidden threshold. And Jesus welcomed her without reserve.

She...kissed them and poured perfume on them (Luke 7:38).

As I mentioned before, in this culture women kept their hair bound. To let one's hair down in public was a scandal and grounds for divorce. Loose, flowing hair was considered seductive and reserved only for a husband in the privacy of his own home. But this woman didn't care about society's rules. All she cared about was worshipping Jesus. Using her dark tresses as a hand towel, she dried His feet from her tears.

But she wasn't quite finished. She had one more act of worship to perform. Extravagantly, she cracked the neck of the alabaster jar and poured the entire contents over Jesus' feet. Not only did the fragrance fill the room, but also I imagine everyone at the party carried the fragrance home with them.

She is a sinner (Luke 7:39).

Simon was not too happy with the intrusion of this well-known sinful woman. He certainly was disappointed in Jesus' reaction to her.

Jesus knew what Simon was thinking. All through the New Testament we read of Jesus knowing people's thoughts. After Jesus forgave the paralytic's sins, Mark records that Jesus knew in His spirit what the onlookers were thinking in their hearts (Mark 2:8). When Jesus healed the man with the withered hand on the Sabbath in front of the Pharisees, He "knew what they were thinking" (Luke 6:8). And even though a hush fell on this room of men watching this weeping woman worship at Jesus' feet, the Master knew every word not spoken.

SIMON, DO YOU SEE THIS WOMAN?

Simon doubted Jesus' divinity because He allowed this sinner to touch Him, as if He didn't know what sort of less than woman she was. Jesus proved His divinity by responding to Simon's unspoken thoughts. Not only did Jesus know what kind of woman she was, but also He knew what kind of man Simon was. Simon thought Jesus should have corrected the woman, but instead Jesus corrected him.

> "Simon, I have something to tell you."
>
> "Tell me, teacher," he said.
>
> "Two people owed money to a certain moneylender. One owed him five hundred denarii, and the other fifty. Neither of them had the money to pay him back, so he forgave the debts of both. Now which of them will love him more?"
>
> Simon replied, "I suppose the one who had the bigger debt forgiven."
>
> "You have judged correctly," Jesus said. Then he turned toward the woman and said to Simon, "Do you see this woman?" (Luke 7:40-44).

Let's stop and think about five little words that changed this woman's life. "Do you see this woman?" In her book *Bad Girls of the Bible*, Liz Curtis Higgs points out that "Simon had seen her, but only for *what* she was, not *who* she was. He had looked at her form but not her face. He had eyed her actions but not looked her in the eye and connected with her, human to human."[1]

Simon saw a sinner. Jesus saw a repentant child of God. Jesus saw her…the real her. He looked past the sullied reputation and saw the sincere heart. Our God is El Roi, "the God Who Sees," and He saw this precious woman for all she was and all she could be.

She knew rejection. She knew what it was like to be invited to a party only to be used by the men present there. Jesus understood that as well—He was surrounded by people who only saw what they could squeeze out of Him rather than who He really was. That's why He was invited to Simon's party in the first place. He was an enigma, a curiosity piece, a celebrity on display.

All her life men had used her and women had accused her. But Jesus welcomed her worship and honored her humility. Not once did He recoil or refuse her touch.

Jesus wasn't finished with Simon.

> I came into your house. You did not give me any water for my feet, but she wet my feet with her tears and wiped them with her hair. You did not give me a kiss, but this woman, from the time I entered, has not stopped kissing my feet. You did not put oil on my head, but she has poured perfume on my feet. Therefore, I tell you, her many sins have been forgiven—as her great love has shown. But whoever has been forgiven little loves little (Luke 7:44-47).

Simon invited Jesus to dinner but then paid little attention to Him. The religious leaders made a good show, but they forgot to acknowledge the honored guest. This happens all the time in churches around the world. People get caught up in the service and programs and forget to acknowledge and worship the honored guest—if He's invited at all.

But not so with this woman. She hadn't forgotten Him at all. A woman. A sinful woman. A social outcast.

Perfume was very expensive and hard to come by in those days. Most originated from plant sources, none of which naturally grew in the Holy Land. They had to be imported from Arabia, Iran, India, and elsewhere. Hosts often put a few drops of oil on their guests' heads as a show of hospitality. I imagine it certainly helped the smell of a room full of people who lacked the conveniences of indoor plumbing and daily showers. But this woman did not simply dole out a few drops of costly nard on Jesus' head. She poured out the entire vial. All of it.

It was a scene of contrasts:

- Simon did not welcome Jesus with the customary kiss. The woman had not stopped kissing Jesus' feet since the time she entered.

- Simon did not offer water to wash Jesus' feet. The woman washed His feet with her tears.

- Simon did not put the traditional oil on his guest's head. The woman poured an entire vial on His feet.

- Simon looked on with condemnation. The woman overflowed with love.

- Simon did not give Jesus anything. The woman gave all she had.

This woman asked for nothing but received everything. She found healing in the home of a hypocrite.

As with the woman at the well, Jesus shone the spotlight on a woman to teach what true worship looks like. As the woman's tears cleansed Jesus' feet, His words cleansed her soul: "Your sins are forgiven" (Luke 7:48). It was not what she did that saved her, but rather what she believed. She didn't say a word, but her actions spoke volumes. Jesus knew what was in her heart just as surely as He knew what was in Simon's.

Paul wrote, "It is by grace you have been saved, through faith—and this is not from yourselves, it is the gift of God—not by works, so that no one can boast" (Ephesians 2:8-9). Remember, grace is a gift we don't deserve or earn. We receive it by faith. She didn't earn salvation by her actions but received the gift by faith.

Finally, Jesus said, "Go in peace." Peace follows forgiveness every time.

UNASHAMED

Several years ago, I was teaching at a women's conference. During the times when I was not speaking, I sat in the crowd with the attendees. In one particular session, a gal named Lisa sat in front of me. During the worship times, Lisa raised her hands and praised God as if the two of them were the only ones in the room. "Thank You, Jesus!" she cried at various intervals.

Some were bothered by this outward demonstration of praise. Others wore a knowing smile.

Later, I chatted with Lisa and she told me her story. "I took my first drink when I was 13, lost my virginity at 14, and smoked marijuana for the first time that same year," she began. "For the next 28 years I chased after anything and everything to numb the pain in my life and transport me to a different world…if only temporarily. After high school, I worked as a bartender and was beaten by my boyfriend on a regular basis. Eventually, I started using cocaine. Cocaine is very expensive, and I needed a way to support my habit, so I became a prostitute. With every trick, a part of me died. Eventually, I became numb to it all. Amazingly, I was arrested for writing bad checks, not prostitution. My attorney got me out of jail and into a recovery program. While I was there, I met Jesus Christ. It was Jesus who set me free, and that's the only reason I am alive today."[2]

When I met Lisa, she was a married mother of two and serving as a women's ministry director in a growing and vibrant church. Now tell me, does she have something to praise God about? Absolutely! I can almost see her now walking through the sea of faces, kneeling at Jesus' feet, washing them with her tears, and drying them with her hair. Then breaking the vial and pouring the perfumed oil on His feet.

I can also see Jesus laying His hand on her head and saying the words, "Your sins are forgiven. Your faith has saved you. Go in peace."

Maybe you've not been redeemed from a life of prostitution or drug addiction, but you and I both have been redeemed from a life of sin and condemnation just the same. We all make mistakes…just different ones. The church is full of men and women who look back on the past with some regret. One poor choice: a walk into an abortion clinic, a one-night stand at a college party, a click on the computer keyboard. But no matter how far we've fallen or how well we think we've hidden what we've done, God still sees us. God still loves us. God still welcomes us into His presence.

You are never less than because of your past mistakes and failures. Jesus made sure of that. "Your sins are forgiven. Your faith has saved you. Go in peace."

CHAPTER 7

Welcomed

No Girls Allowed

M ary and Martha lived in a home with their brother, Lazarus, in the small Judean village of Bethany. Bethany was two miles east of the temple in Jerusalem, on the east slope of the Mount of Olives—the final stop on the road from Jericho to Jerusalem. *Bethany* means "house of dates and figs," the perfect place to stop for a little rest and hospitality. Mary and Martha's home often served as a safe haven and quiet retreat for Jesus as He traveled from place to place.

Mary takes center stage three times in Jesus' earthly ministry. Let's sit in the room with Jesus, His disciples, and Lazarus when she steps in the spotlight the first time. The welcome mat is freshly swept, the aroma from the kitchen is wafting from the windows, and the chatter from the group of men lets us know that friends are enjoying a bit of a reprieve.

Mary and Martha were busy in the kitchen making dinner for their honored guest and His friends. "Mary, check on the roasting lamb," Martha called among the clattering of the pots and pans. "And where's the wine? The bread needs kneading in fifteen minutes. The dates need another stir. The olives need the pits removed. And look at those spots on the goblets! There's just so much to do!"

"I'll take a bowl of fresh grapes to the guests," Mary said. "That will give them something to nibble on while we finish the preparations."

As Mary entered the room, she heard Jesus talking about the kingdom of God, the plan of redemption, the fulfillment of prophecy, the forgiveness of sins, and eternal life.

"Do not judge, and you will not be judged," Jesus taught. "Do not condemn, and you will not be condemned. Forgive, and you will be forgiven. Give, and it will be given to you.

"The kingdom of God is like a mustard seed, which a man took and planted in his garden. It grew and became a tree, and the birds of the air perched in its branches."

Jesus noticed Mary standing in the doorway and motioned for her to join them. Looking directly at her, He continued, "The kingdom of God is like yeast that a woman took and mixed into a large amount of flour until it worked all through the dough."

Jesus continued teaching about who He was and what He came to do. Mesmerized by the Rabbi's words, Mary sank to the floor and sat right at the Master's feet with the others. The men shifted uncomfortably in their places, but Jesus lowered His eyes and began speaking directly to Mary—His newest student.

The disciples waited for Jesus to send Mary back into the kitchen where she belonged, but He didn't. They were confused when Jesus welcomed her in the classroom, but they tried their best not to become distracted by her presence. After all, women were not allowed to sit and learn from a rabbi's teaching. They weren't even allowed to join men in such a gathering at all.

Twenty minutes passed before Martha huffed, "Where is that girl!" She angrily stomped into the gathering room with mixing bowl in hand. All eyes turned toward the frustrated sister as she interrupted Jesus and pointed her wooden spoon in Mary's direction.

"Lord," she began sternly, "can't You see that Mary has left me all alone in the kitchen? What does she think she's doing? Don't You care that I have to do all this work by myself while my irresponsible sister is out here lollygagging about? Why, she's not even supposed to be out here at all. It isn't proper for a woman to join a room full of men, much less sit at a rabbi's feet while he's teaching. Put her in her place! Tell her to get back in the kitchen this instant!"

The men turned their heads from Jesus to the red-faced Martha and back to Jesus again.

"Martha, Martha," Jesus replied, "don't get so worked up. Mary is right where she needs to be. You are so worried, bothered, and distracted with the details of living that you miss the joys of life. You don't need to work so hard to fix such an elaborate meal. That's not even important. What *is* important is that I am here and have something to share with you. Mary has figured that out. She has chosen what is important, and I am not going to send her away. She has joined the classroom to learn—to become a disciple of God's Word—and I am not going to take that away from her."

Martha put her flour-covered hand on her hip, spun on her heels, and marched back into the kitchen. "Well, I never," she mumbled as she stomped away.

SITTING AT THE FEET
OF RABBI JESUS

Several facets of this story just tickle me. Call me mischievous, but I get the giggles thinking about Martha trying to put Mary in her place, and then Jesus putting Martha in hers. Let's take a closer look as Luke tells the story.

*A woman named Martha opened her home to him
(Luke 10:38).*

Most likely, because Martha's name was mentioned first, she was the older of the two sisters and hostess for the evening. Luke didn't mention it here, but Martha and Mary had a brother named Lazarus, whom we will later discover was one of Jesus' closest friends.

*She had a sister called Mary, who sat at the Lord's feet
(Luke 10:39).*

So we can fully understand the incredible freedom Jesus offered Mary of Bethany by welcoming her to sit at His feet and join the teaching, let's review how women were viewed in that particular culture.

Remember, during this time in history, women were not allowed to be taught by the rabbis. In the ancient synagogues, women were permitted to listen, but only men were expected to learn. It was a common belief that teaching women was a waste of time because they were incapable of learning.[1]

Josephus, a noted Jewish historian, wrote that a woman "is in every respect less worth than a man!"[2] Women were put in a category with children and slaves. They were viewed as incapable of comprehending religious matters. Rabbi Eliezer ben Azariah taught, "It is better that the words of the law should be burned than that they should be given to a woman."[3] This was the general attitude toward women during Mary and Martha's day. Does that make you sad or mad? I think both responses are appropriate.

In our culture, to sit at someone's feet conjures up a picture of children gathered around the feet of a storyteller or teacher. However, to the first-century Jew, to sit at someone's feet was to take the position of a student being taught. It was a sign of respect and readiness to learn, and it was the position of higher learning. Often teachers sat on a raised platform and students clustered below on the floor. Paul referred to this position when he announced to a hostile crowd that he was taught "at the feet of Gamaliel" (Acts 22:3 KJV).

When Luke tells us Mary was sitting at Jesus' feet, the first-century reader would have understood that she was taking the position of a student in a classroom right along with the men. This was unheard of. It simply was not done.

But Jesus came to liberate women from the religious gender prejudice that kept them from theological studies. Jesus invited women to learn about the One who loved them most—to become theologians in their own right. Mary was an *ezer* who needed to be readied for battle. Jesus was teaching and equipping her for the greatest battle ever fought, and she was an eager soldier volunteering for active duty.

Lord, don't you care that my sister has left me to do the work by myself? (Luke 10:40).

Amazingly, it was not the men who complained. It was Mary's own sister—another woman. Martha was the one who caused the ruckus. "Tell her to get back in here and help me!" she complained.

Martha was mad, and I can understand that. One Thanksgiving I had 38 people for dinner. I would have been fit to be tied if I had been left to serve all those people by myself. I understand her frustration. But I love Martha so much, we're going to let her have a chapter all to herself. Let's stick with Mary for the moment.

Mary has chosen what is better (Luke 10:42).

Boy, was Martha surprised when Jesus applauded Mary's choice to join Him in the classroom. An all-male classroom, I might add. Women had been sequestered in the kitchen for far too long. Jesus invited Mary to put down the pots and pans and pick up paper and pen. He assured His newest pupil and Martha—and you and me, for that matter—that Mary was not out of order. She was exactly where she needed to be.

By reprimanding Martha, Jesus sends a clear message to us all. Life is crammed with activities we deem necessary, but knowing Jesus supersedes everything else that shouts for our attention. As Carolyn Custis James puts it, "More than simply granting women permission to learn as his disciples, Jesus calls Mary, Martha, and the rest of us to make knowing God our highest priority."[4]

ANOINTING THE HEAD OF THE SAVIOR JESUS

We'll get to Mary's second scene in the next chapter, but for now, let's skip ahead to her third scene. Once again, we find Jesus at a dinner party. As usual, the men are gathered around the table and the women are absent. That is until Mary enters the room…again. Only this time she is not there to learn. She is there to teach.

Martha and Mary were hosting a dinner party for Jesus and His closest friends. The party was not at their home, but Simon had convinced Martha to be in charge of the kitchen at his. After all, no one was better at party details than Martha.

But this was a special celebration—no ordinary dinner party. Only months before, Martha and Mary had been mourning their brother Lazarus's death. And now they were celebrating his resurrected life! Lazarus sat alive and well with Jesus and his friends. He was most likely laughing and telling jokes as though he'd never been buried in a dead man's tomb for four days.

"Mary, don't forget to stir the lamb stew," Martha called from across the room. "Our guests will be here any minute."

How kind of Simon the Leper to open his home to us, Mary mused. *Oh, we must do something about his name. After all, he doesn't have leprosy anymore. Jesus healed him months ago. Just look at his skin—smooth as a newborn babe's. If he were still Simon the Leper, none of us would be here,* she chuckled to herself.

As Mary continued to stir the stew, her mind stirred with memories of Jesus' past three years: the helpless healed, the demon-possessed delivered, the rotting raised, the rejected restored, and the sinner saved. But Mary's soaring heart grew heavy as she remembered Jesus' words about His imminent death: "The Son of Man will be betrayed to the chief priests and the teachers of the law. They will condemn Him to death and will turn Him over to the Gentiles to be mocked and flogged and crucified. On the third day He will be raised to life!"

I know our time with Him is short, she thought. *I can't bear the thought of losing Him, and yet, I know that is why He came. That is what He has taught us all along. My heart hurts. What can I do to honor Him?*

Mary's mind traveled to another incident in Jesus' life. She had not witnessed it personally, but she savored the telling and retelling of the day when a sinful woman washed Jesus' feet with her tears and then anointed them with pure nard. It was a different dinner party hosted by a different Simon.

Suddenly, she knew what she had to do.

"Martha, I'll be right back," Mary called.

Mary ran home and went to the secret place where her most valuable treasure was stored. She reached toward the top shelf and lifted the expensive jar of nard perfume. She had been saving the nard for her wedding day, but this was more important. *I want to honor Jesus. He has welcomed me as a disciple, loved me like a sister, taught me as a student, and given me my brother back from the grave. It is the least I can do. I know His time on earth is coming to an end. I want to honor Him now.*

Beaming with anticipation, Mary ran back to Simon's home with passion and purpose. This time the disciples were not shocked when Mary entered the room of men. After three years, they had grown accustomed to Jesus ignoring the man-made rules to honor the God-made women.

Mary carefully moved through the room and hit her mark. She

stopped where Jesus reclined at the table. She snapped off the neck of the alabaster jar and poured the entire pound of nard on Jesus' head and feet. Even as she poured out the perfume, a sadness seeped into her soul. It was a knowing.

Some looked on the anointing with understanding and approval. Some turned up their noses in pious protest.

"What a waste," one of the disciples complained. "That perfume could have been sold at a high price and the money given to the poor."

Jesus heard Judas' words, and Mary didn't even care. "Why are you bothering this woman?" Jesus asked while placing His hand on her head. "She has done a beautiful thing to Me. You'll always have the poor to take care of, but you will not always have Me here with you. Don't you get it? When she poured this perfume on My body, she did it to prepare Me for burial. She didn't just pour it on My feet like before, but on my head. I tell you the truth," Jesus announced loud enough for all to hear, "wherever this gospel is preached throughout the world, what Mary has done will also be told."

Jesus smiled as His eyes met Mary's.

PREPARING THE BODY
OF SACRIFICIAL JESUS

This account of Mary of Bethany anointing Jesus is recorded in three of the four Gospels: Matthew 26:6-13; Mark 14:3-9; John 12:1-8. We'll blend all three together to take a closer look.

Luke 7:37 also records an incident of a woman anointing Jesus at a dinner party, but this is clearly a different incident. The Luke account occurred at a Pharisee's home, and the woman honoring Jesus was referred to as a "sinful" woman. This incident is at Simon the Leper's home, and John makes it clear that the woman is Mary. So two different Simons: Simon the Pharisee in Luke 7 and Simon the Leper in John 12, Matthew 26, and Mark 14.

Six days before the Passover, Jesus came to Bethany, where Lazarus lived, whom Jesus had raised from the dead. Here a dinner was given in Jesus' honor (John 12:1-2).

While Jesus was in Bethany in the home of Simon the Leper (Matthew 26:6).

The news of Lazarus' resurrection had fueled the Pharisees' determination to put Jesus to death. Jesus no doubt sensed the ominous cloud approaching, and while the partygoers celebrated with gaiety, Jesus pondered the days ahead.

From the blending of these two passages, we learn that Jesus was at a dinner party in Simon the Leper's home. How would you like that name? "Sharon the Leper." But this was no ordinary leper. This was a healed leper. Had he not been healed, he wouldn't have been hosting a dinner party but instead been keeping away from people yelling, "Unclean! Unclean!" A better name for this fellow would have been "Simon the Healed Leper."

Imagine the healed leper with skin as clear as a baby's bottom sharing a carafe of wine with the resurrected dead man—Lazarus. I would have loved that party! And yet, when I think about it, every time we sit around the table with other Christians, we are sharing a meal with the once spiritually dead who are now spiritually alive. That *is* reason to celebrate!

The party was at Simon's home, but Martha and Mary were in charge of the dinner details. John 12:2 tells us, "Martha served." No surprise there. Doesn't that just make you smile? Who better than Martha to be cooking up the food? Listen, I love Martha. We'll see why she's one of my all-time favorites in the next chapter.

Lazarus was among those reclining at the table with him (John 12:2).

During dinner parties or banquets such as this one, guests did not sit at tables with chairs but reclined on floor cushions placed around the perimeter of low-lying tables. Their heads were near the table, while they leaned on one arm and ate with the other. With His legs tucked behind Him, Jesus' feet would have been easily accessible.

Mary took about a pint of pure nard, an expensive perfume (John 12:3).

While the NIV translation uses the word *pint* of pure nard, the original Greek word is *litran*, which literally means "pound." The ESV translates the same word "pound" of pure nard, referring to the Roman pound, which is about 12 ounces—no little amount. Mark tells us that the perfume was contained in an alabaster jar (Mark 14:3). The jar was most likely a sealed flask with a long neck. Mary could have easily broken the bottle's neck to pour out the oil.

Matthew and Mark recorded that she anointed Jesus' head; John noted that she also anointed His feet, but Jesus said, "She poured perfume on my body" (Mark 14:8; see also Matthew 26:12). While the disciples noticed the places the perfume touched, Jesus pointed out the purpose. She wasn't merely anointing His head or His feet; she was preparing His body for burial.

Even though this was a party, I imagine Jesus was thinking about what was about to happen in just a few short days. He would come face-to-face with evil, and even though He knew He would win the war, the battle would be painfully fierce. And then here came sweet Mary. She came not only to honor Jesus for who He was, but also for what He would become—the supreme sacrifice for all our sins.

Author Carolyn Custis James notes:

> While everyone else retreated and denied, even tried to set up road blocks to deter him from his mission, Mary came alongside and urged him forward. As darkness descended over Bethany and the shadow of the cross fell across his path, she alone encouraged him to obey his Father. She

alone said yes to the cross. It is a stunning moment, for Mary, and for us.[5]

Those closest to Jesus failed to understand His prediction of His death and resurrection. They were too busy arguing about who was the greatest among them and vying for the best seat in the heavenly kingdom. But Mary of Bethany understood and took action to prepare Jesus in the only way she could.

The nard was most likely Mary's dowry—for her future husband. When Mary let down her hair, this was also an act reserved for a woman's husband. How precious that Mary understood that Jesus was indeed her heavenly Bridegroom.

She saw a need and met it. But I wonder if her actions and Jesus' response to it made the others in the room wonder, "Why didn't I think of that?" The same reaction took place when Jesus wrapped a towel around His waist and began washing His disciples' feet in John 13. "Here, let me do that," Peter said.

Oh, that we would shed our hesitations and inhibitions in worship. I never want to regret a missed opportunity and say, "Why didn't I think of that?" when it comes to serving Jesus.

Judas Iscariot, who was later to betray him, objected (John 12:4).

Here's how John puts it:

> The house was filled with the fragrance of the perfume. But one of his disciples, Judas Iscariot, who was later to betray him, objected. "Why wasn't this perfume sold and the money given to the poor? It was worth a year's wages." He did not say this because he cared about the poor but because he was a thief; as keeper of the money bag, he used to help himself to what was put into it (John 12:3-6).

Nard is fragrant oil made from the spikenard plant grown in northern India. As Judas pointed out, the amount Mary used was worth a year's wages. He was not happy with her act of worship. It rubbed him the wrong way—not because he was concerned about the poor but because he was thinking about his pocket.

In Matthew's account of this story, it was after this dinner party that Judas went to the chief priests and offered to hand over Jesus for 30 pieces of silver. When someone has turned their back on God, nothing riles them more than a person who loves God with all her heart.

Why are you bothering this woman? (Matthew 26:10).

It seems Jesus was always defending Mary. Whether taking up for her with her contentious sister or defending her in front of a group of burly men, Jesus respected Mary's choices and honored her actions.

Just a few days earlier, Jesus took the disciples aside and told them what was about to happen:

> "We are going up to Jerusalem," he said, "and the Son of Man will be delivered over to the chief priests and teachers of the law. They will condemn him to death and will hand him over to the Gentiles, who will mock him and spit on him, flog him and kill him. Three days later he will rise" (Mark 10:33-34; see also Luke 18:31-33).

But the disciples didn't get it. Perhaps they didn't *want* to get it. Perhaps they simply couldn't grasp the idea of anything other than Jesus becoming a ruler over Jerusalem. Luke says that the truth was "hidden from them" (18:34). It could have been that God closed their eyes to the truth until the fulfillment had occurred. We aren't sure.

Through the years, many have viewed Mary's act as accidentally prophetic—as a sweet gesture. It is a mistake to think women in the Bible acted in powerful ways accidently—that they had no idea as to the significance of their actions. I believe Mary knew exactly what she was doing. While others in the room seemed unclear about the details of Jesus' impending death and resurrection, Mary seemed to have understood its coming. She knew what she was doing and why she was doing it. Jesus said as much: "She did this in preparation for my burial" (John 12:7 NLT). Mary the student was now Mary the teacher. Mary of Bethany's actions opened the door for women to sit at the feet of Rabbi Jesus and become Bible students, scholars, and teachers.

What she has done will also be told, in memory of her (Matthew 26:13).

There are few incidences in the New Testament where Jesus shone a spotlight on a particular person and said to everyone around, including you and me, "Take a look at this. This is important." Jesus took no chances that we would soon forget Mary of Bethany's prophetic actions and highlighted them for both then and now.

TEACHING THE TRUTHS OF THE TEACHER

I've had several female friends who have attended seminary and earned masters and doctoral degrees. One told me of a time when she was studying in the school library when a professor walked over with more than a hint of mischief in his eyes and said, "You know, there have never been any great women theologians." His casual remark left its mark on this student of God's Word, and she began a journey to prove him wrong. Rather than discourage and dampen the enthusiasm of this five-foot, four-inch dynamo, the professor lit a fuse that released the power God had intended all along.

The professor was wrong. There have been many great women theologians, and in this chapter, we met one of the first: Mary of Bethany.

Why are we taught? To keep knowledge to ourselves? That certainly wasn't Jesus' model in the New Testament. Jesus taught His disciples so they could in turn go out and teach others. Timothy wrote, "All Scripture is God-breathed and is useful for teaching, rebuking, correcting and training in righteousness, so that [all God's people] may be thoroughly equipped for every good work" (2 Timothy 3:16-17). God's Word is not a secret treasure meant to be hoarded for our sole benefit. God's Word is discovered treasure meant to be invested into the lives of others.

God calls women, right along with men, to be runners (Hebrews 12:1-2), warriors (Ephesians 6:10-18), ambassadors (2 Corinthians 5:20), teachers (Acts 18:26), prophets (Acts 2:17), and workers (Ephesians 2:10). And He calls us to be equipped by being students of His Word (2 Timothy 3:16-17).

As I sit at my computer, I am surrounded on every side with shelves filled with books written by men *and* women theologians. My heart swells with effervescent joy when I look at the titles penned by some of my dearest friends—sisters in Christ who accepted God's call on their lives to be taught by Him and then to teach others about Him. Without their courage, I would most likely not be writing this book today.

We first met Mary as she walked into the classroom and became a student. But in her final scene, she turned the tables and taught those around her. She didn't do it with her words, but with her actions. Jesus served as her interpreter and explained her prophetic message. "She did what she could," Jesus told the disciples.

Mary knew she was powerless to stop the evil that was about to be unleashed against Jesus. But she could do this. She could honor Him with what she had right then. She could prepare Him for burial before He faced the cross. Her tears let us know she understood that the time for Him to die was near. This was not a celebratory offering. She was not joyful but mournful. Her actions were prophetic in the greatest sense.

Let's go back to that seminary professor's comment. "You know, there have never been any great women theologians." Jesus would disagree. There have been many. He made sure of it. Mary of Bethany was one.

CHAPTER 8

Invited

Head of the Class

Just as with Mary of Bethany, we encounter her sister, Martha, in three separate scenes in the life of Jesus. We've already been a fly on the wall at two dinner parties with Jesus, and she was in the kitchen both times. Now we need to rewind and look at the stories from Martha's point of view. What was going on in her mind? Was Jesus disappointed in Martha? Did she feel less than the men, or even her own sister, Mary? How did Jesus' comment affect her in the long run? Let's go back to the first dinner gathering at Martha and Mary's house and join big sister in the kitchen.

"So many details," Martha huffed as she ground wheat into a fine powder. "That Lazarus. He's at it again. He just waltzes in here and announces that Jesus and His friends are stopping by for dinner. Jesus! Not just anyone, but the prophet we've heard so much about. The man who teaches with authority and heals with but a word. Jesus!

"And a few friends? Count them. Jesus plus 12. A dinner party like this takes days to prepare, and Lazarus gives me four hours' notice. There is so much to do: mix the dough, beat the dough, weave the dough, cook the dough; prepare the lamb, roast the lamb, baste the lamb; select the wine, gather the goblets, pull the best plates from storage; sweep the floor, fluff the pillows, scrub the table; dust the furniture, fill the oil lamps, trim the wicks. My head is spinning just thinking of all the details."

"Who are you talking to?" Martha's sister, Mary, asked as she walked into the kitchen.

"I'm talking to myself," Martha answered. "I have much to do to prepare for Jesus' arrival, and I'm counting on you to do your part."

"Don't worry, Martha," Mary consoled. "Everything will be just fine."

Martha worked furiously, preparing all the details and barking out orders to anyone within earshot. And right in the middle of pounding the risen dough, she heard a knock at the door.

"Come on in," she heard her brother welcoming the guests. "We've been waiting for you!"

"Waiting my foot," Martha mumbled. "I'm working myself to death."

The men gathered in the front room and were soon rapt in wonder as Jesus began teaching about the forgiveness of sins and the kingdom of God.

"I'll take a bowl of fresh grapes to the guests," Mary said. "That will give them something to nibble on while we finish the preparations."

"That's fine," Martha agreed. "But come right back."

Minutes passed, but Mary never returned to the kitchen. Finally, Martha peeked into the room and saw her sister sitting at Jesus' feet, taking in every word He said.

Martha angrily stomped into the gathering room with mixing bowl in hand. All eyes turned to the frustrated sister as she interrupted Jesus and pointed her wooden spoon in Mary's direction.

"Lord," she began sternly, "can't You see that Mary has left me all alone in the kitchen? What does she think she's doing? Don't You care that I have to do all this work by myself while my irresponsible sister is out here lollygagging? Why, she's not even supposed to be out here at all. It isn't proper for a woman to join a room full of men, much less sit at a rabbi's feet while he's teaching. Put her in her place! Tell her to get back in the kitchen where she belongs!"

"Martha, Martha," Jesus replied, "don't get so worked up. Mary is right where she needs to be. You are so worried, bothered, and distracted with the details of living that you miss the joys of life. You don't need to work so hard to create a feast for us. That's not even important. What *is* important is that I am here and have something to share with you. Mary has figured that out. She has chosen what is important, and I am not going to send her away. She has joined the classroom to learn—to become a disciple of God's Word—and I am not going to take that away from her."

Martha put her flour-covered hand on her hip, spun around on her heels, and marched back into the kitchen. "Well, I never," she mumbled as she stomped away.

THE DOOR LEFT OPEN

I've often heard that no matter how flat a pancake is, it still has two sides. So let's take a closer look at the famous Mary and Martha story from big sister's point of view.

Tell her to help me! (Luke 10:40).

Did you catch that Martha is telling Jesus what to do? She wants to be in control. Oh, I would never do that. Well...okay, maybe I have done that a time or two...or three. I'm especially guilty of telling Jesus how to straighten out someone else's knotted attitude or behavior.

You are worried and upset about many things (Luke 10:41).

The Greek word Jesus used here is translated "worried," but it can also be translated "distracted." It literally means to drag all around, to pull apart, or to pull away. Another translation states that Martha was "cumbered about much serving" (verse 40 KJV). "Cumbered" implies "drawn away or distracted." The New American Standard Bible says, "Martha, Martha, you are *worried* and *distracted* by many things" (verse 41, emphasis mine). Finally, the Amplified Bible reads: "Martha, Martha, you are worried and bothered *and* anxious about so many things; but *only* one thing is necessary, for Mary has chosen the good part [that which is to her advantage], which will not be taken away from her" (verses 41-42). Simply put, Martha was having a hissy fit about details.

I understand Martha's frustration. As I mentioned earlier, one year I had 38 people for Thanksgiving dinner. If everyone had gathered around the television to watch the Thanksgiving parade while I was left basting the turkey, stirring the gravy, mixing the stuffing, baking the pumpkin pie, steaming the broccoli, and brewing the tea, my emotions would have been basting, stirring, mixing, baking, steaming, and brewing as well. (That was not the case, by the way. Everyone pitched in, and all I had to do was make sure everyone had a place to sit with their mounds of food.) But if we stop there, we are missing the point. This section of Scripture is not about how Martha was feeling at the time, but about what Jesus was inviting her to do in the future.

Jesus didn't just wag His finger at Martha with a "tsk, tsk." No, He used this as a teachable moment. "Martha, Martha," He began. Don't you just love how He addressed her? With love and compassion, He began to teach His lovely friend. His voice didn't have a hint of anger. In effect, He was inviting Martha to become one of His students as well.

Jesus used this teachable moment for Mary, for Martha, and for the disciples. He also used it for you, me, and others who would become students of the Word in the years to come.

Jesus' response was certainly not what Martha expected. I imagine she thought Jesus would have quickly sided with her and pointed Mary back toward the kitchen where she belonged. And his response wasn't what the disciples expected. After all, women were not supposed to be learning with the men but cooking with the women. However, Jesus seldom responded as they expected. Mary was welcomed to sit with the men. Martha was invited too.

Jesus loved Martha just as much as He loved Mary. If she could just put down that mixing bowl and sit down to listen, she would know how much. Meanwhile, Jesus put a lid on her boiling emotions and left her to simmer on what He had said. And I think He left the door open.

What do you think Martha did after she walked back into the kitchen? We are not told. Luke simply goes on to another story and leaves us with Martha holding the spoon and Jesus holding the door.

M.L. del Mastro, in his book *All the Women of the Bible*, retells stories of biblical women in narratives that paint beautiful landscapes with the simple outlines given in the Scriptures. In his story of Martha, he writes that Martha was freed from "the imprisoning, lethal order she craved, so that she could live." He went on to say:

> After that amazing meal, order gradually became less and less her god, less the air she needed for breathing, and more simply a product of her active giving and receiving of love. She learned to relax and let other people do what they did best without feeling challenged or threatened, because she learned that she could be, was in fact, loved for who she was, not for what she did and how she did it. That was how her service was becoming service in reality, not just a disguise for control nor a means to prevent her own annihilation. That "better part" became her choice as well, thanks to Him.[1]

Have you ever wondered why the story of Martha steamed up in the kitchen was included in Luke's Gospel in the first place? It's not about a healing, deliverance, or absolution of sin. It is not one of Jesus' parables or related to His journey to the cross. I believe the story is included as an example of how Jesus came to set women free—free to become His disciples, to sit at His feet, and to join the classroom that had previously been reserved for men only. I believe it is included to help women see just what is truly important in this life.

So what did Martha do after she walked back in the kitchen? I'll tell you what I think she did. I think she stewed a bit more—maybe for the rest of the day. But at some point, Martha took Jesus up on His invitation to join Him in the classroom. She became a disciple as well. How do I know? Because of the pop quiz she was about to take in her next New Testament appearance.

POP QUIZ ON THE ROAD

Mary and Martha were women just like us with daily trials and triumphs, past regrets and remorse, and future hopes and dreams. Yet even though our hearts may be the same, their culture was very different. Single women in those days, whether never married or widowed, depended on their brothers or fathers to take care of them. They didn't usually work outside the home, and no welfare system existed to take care of the disenfranchised. Retirement plan? That would be a brother or son. For these two women, Lazarus was all they had. If he died, their support died with him. In our second encounter with the sisters, that is the very cliff upon which their futures teeter. Let's join them now at their dying brother's bedside.

"Martha," Mary cried, "what are we going to do? We've tried everything, yet Lazarus' skin is still so hot. Even cold water fails to lower his fever. His eyes are glazed, his tongue is like dried leather, and he no longer responds to our voices."

Martha's strong brother never got sick. But this sickness had come over him so quickly, and nothing they did seemed to help. His body burned with fever and only cooled temporarily when bathed in the well water. He hadn't eaten for days and only drank when she could force him to take a few sips.

"We have one hope left," Martha decided. "Someone needs to go and get Jesus. He could heal him by just saying the word."

"That's it!" Mary cried. "I'll send someone right away!" She called out to a trusted friend who paced in the yard, waiting for word of his friend's health. "Daniel! Go get Jesus. We need Him right away. Last I heard He was teaching by the Jordan."

"What shall I tell Him?" Daniel asked.

"Tell Him, 'The one You love is sick,'" she replied. "He'll know what to do."

So off Daniel ran to find the Master. But only moments after Daniel left Bethany, Lazarus took a turn for the worse and breathed his last.

When Daniel arrived and gave Jesus the news, the Teacher did not respond as the messenger had expected. Even His disciples were surprised by His seeming lack of concern. "This sickness is not the end of Lazarus. It's for God's glory," Jesus replied. The disciples didn't understand many of Jesus' statements, and this one left them scratching their heads.

Jesus didn't pick up and go to His friend right away. Rather, He stayed at the camp for two more days. Then, on the third day, God signaled it was time to go. By the time Jesus reached the city limits, Lazarus had been dead four days, and his body was sealed away in the cavelike tomb.

Martha's home was loud with wailing and heavy with grief. When someone whispered to Martha that Jesus was only a short distance away, she jumped up and ran to meet Him.

"Lord," Martha cried as she fell at Jesus' feet, "if You had been here, this would not have happened. Lazarus would not have died. Where were You? Why didn't You come?" As quickly as the accusations spilled out of her mouth, she tried to take them back. "But I know that even now God will give You whatever You ask."

Jesus placed His hand on Martha's shoulder and quietly spoke. "Your brother will rise again."

"I know he will rise again in the resurrection at the last day," she responded.

Jesus continued, "I am the resurrection and the life. If anyone believes in Me, he will live, even if he dies. Martha, do you believe this?"

"I do, Lord," she replied. "I believe that You are the Son of God, whose coming was promised to us."

Jesus' heart soared with pride at Martha's words. While so many of His closest friends didn't understand who He was and what He came to do, Martha got it. She passed the pop quiz with flying colors and moved to the head of the class. Oh, how He loved her!

"Martha, go and get Mary for Me. I want to talk to her too."

Martha ran back to the house full of weeping neighbors and whispered in Mary's ear. "Jesus is here. He's asking for you."

Mary leapt to her feet and rushed out the door. Many of the mourners thought Mary was running to the tomb in a surge of grief and followed after her. But she wasn't running to the tomb; she was running to the Teacher. When she arrived, Mary fell at Jesus' feet just like her sister had done and spoke the words her sister had spoken: "Oh Lord, if You had been here, my brother would not have died. Why didn't You come? Where have You been?"

When Jesus saw her broken heart, His eyes filled with tears. Oh, how He hated death—the curse of Eden. How He loathed the result of sin and Satan's sting. He was so overcome with emotion and love for this family that He couldn't even offer a word of condolence. He simply wept.

"Where have you laid him?" Jesus asked.

"Come and see," she replied.

When Jesus arrived at the tomb, salty tears fell from the face of the God-made man and wet the cursed ground on which He stood.

Jesus surveyed the crowd and caught the eye of two strapping young men. "Take the stone away from the mouth of the cave," He instructed them.

"But, Lord," Martha said, "Lazarus has been in the tomb for four days. His body will have started to decay. There will be a terrible stench."

"Martha, trust Me. Didn't I tell you that if you believed you would see the glory of God?" He replied. So the men rolled away the stone as the crowd held their breath in anticipation. Jesus prayed aloud and then called out in a loud voice toward the tomb. "Lazarus, come out!"

A low hanging cloud of silence stilled the air. And then…a linen-bound man appeared at the tomb's opening.

Gasps, cheers, and cries of joy broke the silence, and the mourning turned to dancing.

"Unbind him and let him go," Jesus instructed.

DEATH DEFIED.
RESURRECTION DEFINED.

Have you ever sat by someone's bedside and watched his or her life slip away? It's a helpless feeling. There is nothing you can do as the body begins to shut down like the lights going out in a tall building. I am sure the sisters did everything they knew to do, and yet nothing helped.

I have never felt that more clearly than when my mother took her last breath. Like Lazarus, it was a quick passing. Not months but weeks. Part of her intestines stopped working and her heart wasn't strong enough to survive surgery. For six precious weeks, I sat by her bed and watched her ebb away. Five weeks into the waiting, she told the doctors to unhook all the tubes. She was ready to go.

For six weeks we laughed; we cried; we waited. Then one morning she simply stopped breathing and left us. When death comes knocking, we humans are powerless to stop its intrusion. But Jesus was about to show the crowd that He is Master over life and death.

Much had happened since Jesus' initial visit in Martha's home. He had opened the eyes of the blind, made the lame to walk, cleansed the lepers' skin, multiplied the bread, and now raised the dead. The small village of Bethany would have received reports of Jesus' teachings and miracles. No matter what the masses thought about who He was, they could not deny what He did. He was taking Martha to a deeper level of understanding—still as her Teacher.

Let's take a closer look at the story as told by John.

Lord, the one you love is sick (John 11:3).

Interestingly, when we met Martha and Mary in our first encounter, no mention was made of their brother, Lazarus. But as the story unfolds, we learn that he was one of Jesus' dearest friends. They weren't less than but equal to their brother when it came to Jesus' affection.

In verse 2 of this passage, John notes Mary pouring perfume on Jesus' feet. However, this had not happened yet. This didn't happen until the week of Jesus' death and resurrection. Here, John gives us a taste of what is yet to come.

John, the disciple who penned this account, often referred to himself as "the one Jesus loved." But here, the sisters refer to their brother in those same endearing terms.

Martha didn't presume to tell Jesus what to do as she did in their kitchen encounter. She simply explained the situation and trusted Jesus to take care of it as He saw best. When it came to healing her brother, she didn't care how He did it, just that He did. Boy, was she in for a surprise—which is often the case when we leave matters in

God's hands to work in the way He chooses, unhindered by our own interference.

If Martha had had a watch, you can believe she would have checked it often. "Where is He?" she must have wondered. "What's taking so long?" Her hope was ebbing away with her brother's waning life.

Jesus loved Martha and her sister and Lazarus
(John 11:5).

Hold everything! This is one of my favorite passages in the entire story. For so long, Martha has gotten a bad rap. Mary has been portrayed as the lovely lady who sat pensively at Jesus' feet and Martha as the grumpy older sister bossing everyone around. In our skewed imaginations, we picture Jesus loving Mary and disapproving of Martha. But read that verse again. "Now Jesus loved Martha and old what's-her-name." I love it! Not because I am *not* a fan of Mary, but because I *am* a fan of Martha, just like Jesus was. Let's keep going, and I'll tell you more about why in a moment.

When he heard that Lazarus was sick, he stayed where
he was (John 11:6).

John might as well be saying, *I just didn't get it. He loved them, but He waited. What's up with that? If He would stop to help a stranger, certainly He would travel to heal a friend.*

Jesus didn't go at once because God had a greater plan. We have the insight of hindsight, but the disciples were simply confused.

It would have been a miracle on a small scale to heal a sick friend, but it was a miracle on a grand scale to raise him from the dead. Waiting on God is a difficult lesson to learn when degenerating circumstances are draining our hope dry, but God wants to make sure we understand that we are absolutely helpless in our own strength so that we will understand His greatness. That's what the disciples were learning to do.

Two days later, God gave the signal. It was time to go.

Not only was it time to go and perform the miraculous resurrection of Lazarus that we know is on the way, but it was also time for Jesus to return to the very area where the Pharisees were seeking to kill Him. There was clear and present danger in His decision to return to Judea. The Pharisees had already tried to stone Him, and Jesus knew they were plotting His death. He also knew they were going to succeed. The end was drawing near, and this monumental miracle would make the Pharisees more determined than ever to get rid of Him.

The disciples warned Jesus not to go back into hostile territory, but Jesus was firm in His resolve. Jesus further confused their thinking by explaining that Lazarus was already dead. To the disciples, traveling to Bethany didn't seem like a wise career move. They didn't see the point. If Lazarus was already dead, why take the chance? To Jesus, it was the next step to accomplishing His ultimate goal.

By the time Jesus arrived, Lazarus' decaying body had been in the tomb for four days. Jewish tradition called for 30 days of mourning, and the wailing was in full swing. This death shook the entire village, and many Jews from surrounding cities came to mourn the loss. For these two women, it was more than the loss of a brother. With no husband, no children, no father, and now no brother, they were left with no one to take care of them in a culture where it was difficult for a woman to provide for her own needs.

If you had been here, my brother would not have died (John 11:21).

Have you ever felt the same way? *Lord, if You had been here, this would not have happened. Where were You? Where are You now?* Martha was disappointed in Jesus. He could have prevented Lazarus' death but hadn't. But as always, Jesus wasn't late. He was right on time.

Martha battled between the realities of her brother's decaying body and the knowledge that Jesus could have prevented it. She's no different from you and me. We often question God when what we expect doesn't match up with what we experience.

Do you think Jesus knew Mary and Martha would be disappointed in Him for not showing up before Lazarus died? Of course He did. But nevertheless, He waited because He was more interested in obeying God than obliging man.

> We often question God when what we expect
> doesn't match up with what we experience.

God will give you whatever you ask (John 11:22).

That was an "oops" moment for Martha. What had been rambling around in her head tumbled out of her mouth. Martha quickly backpedaled and spoke what she *knew* to be true in her head, even though she didn't *feel* it to be true in her heart. She knew Jesus could, even now, raise Lazarus from the dead. He *could* do anything.

Jesus said to her, "Your brother will rise again."

Martha answered, "I know he will rise again in the resurrection at the last day."

Jesus said to her, "I am the resurrection and the life. The one who believes in me will live, even though they die; and whoever lives by believing in me will never die. Do you believe this?" (John 11:23-26).

Do you see what Jesus is doing here? He is teaching Martha the fundamental principle of the gospel: Belief in Jesus leads to eternal life with God. While the disciples were watching, Jesus was teaching a woman...again. This is why I love Martha. She did indeed leave the kitchen and join Jesus in the classroom. She put aside her worrisome ways, her distracting details, and her bossy behavior. After she simmered down, Martha accepted Jesus' invitation to become a disciple in her own right. We don't have the recorded scenes of her sitting at Rabbi Jesus' feet to learn, but it appears she did. She became a stellar student and moved to the head of the class with Mary.

Once again, Jesus tenderly took advantage of a teachable moment and led Martha to a place of deeper understanding. In usual Jesus-style, He did so by asking questions: "Do you believe this?"

This was Martha's pop quiz. Let's see if she passed.

> "Yes, Lord," she replied, "I believe that you are the Messiah, the Son of God, who is to come into the world" (John 11:27).

Martha understood. Her profession of faith during a time when even Jesus' closest friends were unsure is remarkable. She was a magnificent woman of faith who had learned her lessons well. Her words let us know that she did choose what was better and took her seat at the feet of Rabbi Jesus.

God often puts our beliefs through the sifter of difficulties to grind out the lumps of doubt we didn't even know were there. Struggles test our faith and solidify our beliefs. As Peter wrote, trials come so that our faith may be proved genuine (1 Peter 1:7). Martha's theology was solid. She knew what she believed. No hesitation.

God often puts our beliefs through the sifter of difficulties to grind out the lumps of doubt we didn't even know were there.

---

*She went back and called her sister Mary aside
(John 11:28).*

And what was Martha's message for Mary? "The Teacher is here and is asking for you."

The words "Jesus is asking for you" give me chills. Can you imagine someone knocking on your door and saying, "Jesus is asking for you"? The truth is, Jesus does knock on your door and *is* asking for you (Revelation 3:20).

When Mary ran to meet Jesus and fell at His feet, He was so moved He couldn't even offer any words of consolation. He simply asked, "Where have you laid him?" And what happened when Jesus arrived at the tomb surrounded by mourners? Two simple words:

Jesus wept (John 11:35).

The mourners' pain opened a floodgate of emotion in Jesus. He understood Martha and Mary's hurt…and He understands ours as well.

We know the rest of the story. Jesus did indeed raise Lazarus from the dead, and many people put their faith in Him as a result. However, there were some who did not welcome the miracle. Rather, they ran to the Pharisees and gave them more ammunition to crucify Him (John 11:46). Isn't that always the case? In the face of a miracle, our faith will be strengthened or the fight against that faith will become fiercer. We will either choose to believe in God or look for reasons to run from Him.

Martha moved beyond the cultural beliefs that women were less than men and needed to stay within the confines of hearth and home. By her confession of faith after Lazarus' death, we see that she had joined Mary at the feet of Rabbi Jesus. She didn't become *just* a student. She moved to the head of the class.

Jesus never talked down to Martha but gently instructed her. She was not less than the men; she was not less than Mary. Again, He completely reversed the traditional priorities outlined for women of that day and invited her to become a disciple—a student of God's Word. While the culture dictated that women were exempt from learning the Torah, Jesus showed her that learning about God was the best choice of all.

WORSHIPPING GOD IN THE KITCHEN

Our last glimpse of Martha is at Simon the Leper's dinner party, where Mary anointed Jesus' body with perfume and prepared Him for burial. And where is Martha? Why, she's in the kitchen serving. Being a disciple of Jesus Christ does not release us from our day-to-day activities and responsibilities. We still cook dinner, vacuum the house, dust the furniture, go to the office, pay the bills, mow the lawn. But knowing Jesus gives us the freedom to serve joyfully, giving to others out of the overflow of our relationship with the Savior. God didn't change Martha's natural bent toward serving, but He did change her sinful bent toward complaining, projecting her expectations on others, and attempting to control people's actions.

Yes, at this final party, Martha was serving in the kitchen. She wasn't fussing about it, worried, bothered, and distracted because Mary wasn't doing her part. After all, Mary was right where she belonged. This time Martha served with a new attitude of thanksgiving and praise for the One who had set her free. She wasn't less than because her gift was serving; she was hardwired that way. She was part of the body of Christ doing what she did best…but with a different attitude.

She was free to be who God had created her to be.

CHAPTER 9

Set Free

The Bent and Bowed Made Straight

It was another Sabbath day, much like any other. But as Mariah opened her eyes, she had no idea this would be the day that changed her life.

"I'm getting too old for this," Mariah groaned as she twisted her crooked body to roll her stiff frame out of bed. "I wish I could just stay home today, but it is the Sabbath."

She swung her legs over the edge of the bed and dropped her feet onto the cold, hard floor. Her gaze and feet hit the packed dirt surface simultaneously, where both spent their waking hours. "At least in bed I can see the sky and the faces of those I love through the window," she moaned. "But not even an old woman can stay in bed all day."

Mariah was in for another day of looking down at the dirt floor, dusty gravel roads, and the mud-caked feet of passersby. For 18 years she had been bent over by an evil spirit that taunted her day and night. Her infirmity hadn't happened all at once, but had progressed gradually—as if someone were laying bricks on the back of her neck, one by one, day by day. Her back slowly succumbed to the invisible weight, and her spine resembled a mound of earth rather than a tall straight palm. Parallel to the floor. Perpendicular to the sky.

"I am so tired of looking at feet," she moaned, "but at least I can see. I can hear. I can speak. I have much to be thankful for. So today I will go to the synagogue to worship."

Mariah ran a comb through her gnarled gray hair, covered her head with a veil, and slipped sandals on her callused feet. Then her shuffle to the temple began. Her frame prohibited her from looking up to find the women's section of the synagogue, so she just followed the feminine feet to find her seat in the back, behind the partition separating the women from the men.

She couldn't see His face, but she recognized His voice. Jesus was teaching today. As soon as He approached the top step, the crowd stirred. "It's Jesus," they began. "The Teacher and Healer everyone is talking about. It's Jesus!"

Ignoring the buzz, Jesus began to teach. Unlike any other man she had ever heard before, Jesus spoke with authority laced with compassion. For the first time in her life, someone explained the Scriptures in a way that made sense to her. He explained spiritual truths with everyday examples that made His teaching come alive. And for the first time ever, this Teacher used examples that women could relate to: a bowl of flour, a new patch sown on old wineskin, a lost coin.

Oh, I wish I could see His face, she silently prayed.

No sooner had the thought entered her mind than Jesus stopped speaking. She couldn't see Him, but He could see her.

An uneasy hush fell over the room.

"Woman, come forward," He instructed.

Mariah strained to lean back on her bench in order to see whom He was speaking to. "He's talking to *you*," her neighbor whispered. "He's looking right at you."

Mariah wasn't exactly sure what she should do. Jesus was asking her to leave the women's section of the synagogue and walk through the sea of men filling the front. She knew women weren't allowed to step into the men's area, but it was Jesus who was calling her forward. After a few moments of internal struggle, faith overcame fear and Mariah was out of her seat shuffling through the men. She couldn't see their faces, but she could feel their stares.

Women gasped at her courage. Men glared at her audacity. Both parted as Mariah passed through the crowd. After a lengthy lumber, Mariah finally made it to the Teacher—center stage. Jesus bent down, placed His hand on the mountain that had become Mariah's back, and leveled the land. She felt warmth surge through her frozen muscles as years of stiffness melted away. Like a marionette in the hands of a puppeteer, Jesus pulled her up. For the first time in 18 years, the bent reed became a tall cedar. The physical defect that had defined her was gone, and she rose to look into the eyes of the One who had set her free.

"Woman," He spoke, "you are free from your infirmity."

Tears of joy coursed down her weathered cheeks, and the words of the psalmist coursed through her veins. "But thou, O Lord, art a shield for me; my glory, and the lifter up of mine head."

"Thank You, Jesus!" she cried. "Thank You, Jesus!" Mariah twirled and raised her hands, giddy as a child. No longer did she feel like the dirt she was forced to stare at day in and day out. She was free!

CHIN UP

Brokenness comes in many forms. Feeling bent and bowed by the weight of the world takes on varied shapes. We don't have to have a mounded back to know what it feels like to be more comfortable looking at feet rather than eyes. Let's take a closer look at one brave sister who took halted steps towards Jesus and was set free to dance again.

> On a Sabbath Jesus was teaching in one of the synagogues, and a woman was there who had been crippled by a spirit for eighteen years. She was bent over and could not straighten up at all (Luke 13:10-11).

I almost hold my breath when a story begins with: "It was the Sabbath." I know right away that Jesus is about to ruffle some feathers. He constantly broke the *who, what, when, where,* and *how* religious rules to be about His Father's business. In this first sentence we get a hint that He's about to break the rules of *when* and the *who*. It was the Sabbath, and there was a woman…

When Jesus saw her, he called her forward (Luke 13:12).

Herod's Temple stood on a hill overlooking the beautiful city of Jerusalem. It was built by Herod and his sons between 19 BC and 63 AD. While most of it was completed by 9 BC, adornment continued for 72 more years. The structure reflected the religious and societal prejudices of the day, with ascending sets of steps and partitions to separate various people groups. The outer area, the court of the Gentiles, was a general area open to all Jews and God-fearing Gentiles. The next level up was called the court of women, where both Jewish men and women were welcomed. The third tier was called the court of the Israelites, and only ceremonially clean Jewish men were allowed. The fourth set of steps led to the Holy Place, where only the priests could enter. Finally, the fifth level contained the Most Holy Place, where the High Priest entered once a year, on the Day of Atonement. A heavy embroidered curtain hung in front of the Most Holy Place and separated man from the presence of God. Picture it as five levels with the words "greater than" written on steps of each ascending level.

In the Old Testament, the God-designed tabernacle had only three divisions. The outer court for men and women, the Holy Place for the appointed priests, and the Holy of Holies, where only the high priest could enter once a year. According to Deuteronomy 31:12 and Joshua 8:35, all people, both men and women, were encouraged to attend regular readings of the law in the outer court. The divisions we see in Herod's Temple during the time of Christ were not God-ordained, but manmade based on prejudice. While Herod agreed to build a temple for the Jews, he felt the outlined plans in the Torah were much too small to have his name attached to them. So he made a temple larger and grander than God prescribed—including the added levels demeaning the women.

Most likely, the woman in this story was in a local synagogue. While the smaller places of worship didn't have the expansive courtyards and segregated levels that Herod's Temple had, the women would have been sequestered in a separate area from the men. Often a dividing curtain or partition separated the two groups.

As one commentator noted:

> Jesus' invitation to the crippled woman struck out against the male monopoly of public worship. When Jesus put her in the spotlight, right down in front of the whole synagogue, He shattered the men's worldview. There must have been a collective gasp from dignified rows of men that day. Didn't Jesus know what He was doing? Women were supposed to be kept in their place, hidden behind the dividing screens![1]

When Luke tells us that Jesus called her forward, we see Jesus breaking the *where* rule. He called the woman to leave her designated section, walk through the sea of men, and take her place front and center. Jesus called the woman out of the shadows and onto center stage.

And, finally, Luke tells us the *what*.

He put his hands on her, and immediately she straightened up (Luke 13:12-13).

Healed! Just like that.

This is one incident when Jesus did not mention the woman's faith.

In the case of the woman with the 12-year bleeding, Jesus said, "Daughter, your faith has healed you" (Mark 5:34). This time, Jesus didn't mention the woman's faith, but make no mistake about it, she had to take several steps of faith to walk through the forbidden crowd of men to see the One who saw her first. And where those steps took her was enough to make any woman quake in her sandals.

Come and be healed on those days (Luke 13:14).

Not everyone was happy about Jesus miraculously healing this bent and bowed woman. The *who, what, when,* and *where* of the healing riled the synagogue leader. He was more concerned with the binding law than the bound-up woman. This healing was not on the schedule or in the bulletin, so to speak. It was out of order—*their* order.

> Indignant because Jesus had healed on the Sabbath, the synagogue leader said to the people, "There are six days for work. So come and be healed on those days, not on the Sabbath" (Luke 13:14).

A ruler or leader of the synagogue was a layman whose responsibilities were administrative and included such things as looking after the building and supervising worship. Though there were exceptions, most synagogues had only one ruler. Sometimes the title was honorary, with no administrative responsibilities assigned.[2]

So the synagogue leader was a volunteer bouncer. He made sure that everything was done in order and according to the book. *Which* book and *whose* book were debatable.

Interestingly, when the synagogue ruler made his statement of chastisement, he made it to the people, not to Jesus. He turned around and addressed the crowd. "Listen, folks. Strike this miracle from the record. Church is no place for healing. You can get healed on Sunday through Friday, but not on Saturday, the Sabbath. We are here to worship, not get healed."

Imagine this scenario happening in your Sunday morning church service. Right in the middle of the sermon, the pastor steps away from the podium and motions for a woman in a wheelchair to come forward. The woman slowly rolls the chair down the aisle and stops at the edge of the platform.

Then the pastor looks at the woman and says, "Mary, God is healing you today. You are free from your wheelchair. Get up and walk." As the woman rises, for the first time in 18 years, the congregation breaks out in wild applause laced with tears and praises to God.

But then an elder runs forward and addresses the congregation. "Hold everything!" he begins. "This healing was not on the schedule today. It is not printed here in the bulletin. This is not the time and place for healings, Mary. You'll have to come back next week, and we'll write you in."

How crazy would that be! And yet that is the same feeling we get when the synagogue ruler condemns Jesus' actions to the crowd. Because of his sour attitude, he missed the sweet joy of the miracle. He also missed true worship because of his dogged determination to follow man-made rules.

Interestingly, the ruler called the act of healing "work." Work? Did he really call it work? This kind of miracle takes a work of God, but all we have to do is believe and receive. Jesus didn't work up a sweat. And here's the *how* of it all. He touched. He spoke.

> The Lord answered him, "You hypocrites! Doesn't each of you on the Sabbath untie your ox or donkey from the stall and lead it out to give it water? Then should not this woman, a daughter of Abraham, whom Satan has kept bound for eighteen long years, be set free on the Sabbath day from what bound her?" (Luke 13:15-16).

The synagogue leader spoke to the people, but Jesus spoke to him directly. He made a direct correlation between a bound animal and the bound woman. Jesus demonstrated that relationship was more important than religion, people were more important than platitudes, and receptive hearts were more important than repetitive ritual.

Jesus referred to this woman as a "daughter of Abraham." All through the Old Testament, men are referred to as sons of Abraham—men of the covenant. However, this is the first time the Scripture records a woman being referred to as a daughter of Abraham. What was Jesus doing here? He was letting everyone in earshot know that this precious image bearer was not less than her male counterparts. She was just as much a cherished child of God and part of the covenant as any man. No longer was she bent low because of cultural oppression. Now she was raised up because of Jesus' profession.

Here's something else worth noting. Jesus called her "a daughter of Abraham, whom Satan has kept bound for eighteen long years." Who told Jesus she had been bound for 18 years? I don't see that anywhere in the text. Could it be that Jesus knew it had been 18 years because He knew every day of her life? Could it be He knew the days that were marked out for her, the days she would be bent and bowed, and the day she would unbound and free ? I believe so.

> When he said this, all his opponents were humiliated, but the people were delighted with all the wonderful things he was doing (Luke 13:17).

Some praised God for what Jesus had done. Others turned up their pious noses. But she didn't care what anyone thought. She was healed. And you know what? Jesus didn't care what anyone thought either.

BROKEN COMES IN
ALL SHAPES AND SIZES

I was riding down the crowded streets of Mexico City in a cab when I saw her. She measured about four feet high, back curved and bent at the waist at a 90-degree angle. Her gnarled and twisted fingers clung to a dingy brown sack. Like an upside-down chair, her face was parallel to the dirty sidewalk. Feet, dirt, trash. That was her view of the world. She shuffled alongside our car as we inched through congested traffic. I saw her, but she could not see me.

Then God reminded me of the bent and bowed woman we just read about in Luke 13. She wasn't a character in a story, but a real and relevant woman just like you and me. Our sister. God's daughter. We must never forget that. And while we might not be able to relate to being physically compromised in this way, most of us can relate to being emotionally bent and bowed in our own way. We see feet: people passing by going about their busy lives. We see dirt: the mistakes we've made through the years. We see trash: the pain inflicted on us by others and many times by our own poor decisions. And because of that, we feel less than.

Jesus said, "Come to me, all you who are weary and burdened, and I will give you rest. Take my yoke upon you and learn from me, for I am gentle and humble in heart, and you will find rest for your souls" (Matthew 11:28-29). Rest for our souls. Isn't that what we all want? To stop looking at the dirt and start looking at the deliverance available to all of us? To stand up tall and unashamed?

Like this woman, we may have "a spirit of infirmity" as the King James Version calls it (verse 11). A sickness of the soul. That is an interesting way to explain her illness. More than just a crippled back, she had a crippled spirit.

Linda Hollies, in her book *Jesus and Those Bodacious Women,* brings this point home:

> There are many spirits that can cause you to walk around in a bent-over state. They might be your color, your gender, your age, your marital state, your family, or they could be abuse, injustice, resentment, oppression, despair, loneliness, your economic state, or even a physical challenge.

It makes no difference what has hurt you in the past, it makes no difference how old you were when the trauma affected your life, and it makes no difference what your wealth, position, or status is. For the evil one comes to steal, kill, and destroy and each one of us is a candidate for being bent and bowed.[3]

Bent and bowed. The weight of the world on our shoulders. Little by little. Day by day. Heaviness too difficult to bear. A spirit of infirmity. Broken by shame, fear, pain, disappointment, depression, poverty, insecurity, inferiority, inadequacy, or shattered dreams. Satan, the one who orchestrates the spirit of infirmity, wants to bend us into inactivity so that our walk becomes a shuffle, our voice becomes a whisper, our vision becomes a blur.

Who put the chains on her in the first place? Jesus said Satan had her bound (Luke 13:16). All sickness was ushered into the world when Adam and Eve believed Satan's lie over God's truth and ate the forbidden fruit. For the 33 years that Jesus walked the earth, He was in a life-and-death struggle with evil. The battleground is the world, and humans are the pawns of the evil one. Note the language: "locked up" and "set free." This is about much more than physical healing. It is about spiritual freedom. And when Jesus said on the cross, "It is finished," it was. Now, because of Jesus' victory over the enemy through His death and resurrection, we are more than conquerors through faith in Him (Romans 8:37). Never less than, but more than conquerors in every battle we face.

Don't miss this. Jesus said, "Woman, you are *set free* from your infirmity." There are those words again—*set free*. The words paint a picture of chains and manacles falling from a prisoner's shackled body. Another translation says it this way: "Woman, you are *released* from your illness" (Luke 13:12 AMP, emphasis mine). The irons of oppression that held her prisoner to this crippled frame gave way and fell at Jesus' feet as He unlocked the chains that bound her—physically, spiritually, emotionally, culturally.

Jesus came to set us free, and that freedom comes in many forms. Whatever Satan is using to bind you, Jesus gave His life to free you. I can't say that enough. For far too long we've looked at freedom only in terms of what we are free from, but freedom encapsulates so much more than a shedding of chains. Jesus set us free to live the abundant life by being all He has created us to be and accomplishing all He has planned for us to do. Literally setting this infirm woman straight was only the beginning of figuratively setting her straight. She was now at the front of the synagogue, in a place where women were kept at bay. Now what? Do you think she grabbed hold of her healing and then ran back to the women's quarters where she belonged?

We don't know for sure, but I bet she stayed right where she was. I think she sat right down in front of Jesus and continued listening to Him teach just like Mary of Bethany had done. That is, after she danced around praising God until she was breathless. There is much we don't know, but this is what we do know: Jesus did not send her back to the women's portico.

FREEDOM COMES IN
ALL SHAPES AND SIZES

When my brother was a teenager, my mother used to threaten him when he hunched over at the dinner table. "If you don't sit up," she would say, "I'm going to buy you a back brace from Sears." I don't even know if Sears made back braces back then, but it sounded like a pretty good threat to me.

Then I had a son who seemingly grew to six feet overnight. He didn't know what to do with all that height, so he slumped. I tried my best not to say, "If you don't sit up, I'm going to buy you a back brace from Sears."

Then one night my father-in-law took care of it for me. We were measuring and marking various family members' heights on the dining room door frame. My 77-year-old father-in-law, who was about five feet ten, stood with his back against the door frame. Then he took a deep breath and extended his curved back to its fullest upright position. We marked him at six feet three.

I watched Steven's eyes grow wide as Papa grew tall. He saw firsthand the difference it made to stand up straight. Papa was huge, but his bent-over frame hid his once stately stature. Steven caught a glimpse of the strappingly strong man that we had known. From that day on, my son stood straight and tall. I have never seen him slump once since then.

That's what I'm hoping for you. That's why I wrote this book. My hope is that you, upon seeing women who have stood to their full stature, will want to do the same. No more slumping in self-doubt or hunching in half-hearted conviction, but instead standing up to the full stature of a confident woman who knows she is equipped by God, empowered by the Holy Spirit, and enveloped in Jesus Christ. A daughter of Abraham by grafting. A child of God by choosing.

There are many emotions that cause us to slump spiritually and become emotionally bound. Worry wears us down. Regret ruins our confidence. Hatred hardens our hearts. Unforgiveness uglies our souls. Bitterness binds our hearts. Insecurity incapacitates our capabilities.

I was bent low for many years. I listened to words from my past telling me I was ugly, not good enough, and worthless. Inferiority, insecurity, and inadequacy were my three closest companions. I didn't like these three lurking shadows, but they followed me everywhere I went. They stalked me, yelling taunts and accusations that no one heard but me.

The more I listened to them, the more emotionally bound I became. Then one day Jesus called me out of hiding. Called me right up front and center. I didn't want to go, mind you. I had grown comfortable hiding in the back where I felt I belonged. I could hear just fine from my seat along the wall. The lighting wasn't as good, but it was enough to get by.

But then Jesus saw me and called me forward. It wasn't that He hadn't seen me all along. After all, He is El Roi, "the God Who Sees." There was never a day when I had not been in His sight. But now the time had come for Him to set me straight and let me loose. So He called me up front where others could see what He was about to do. Jesus placed His nail-scarred hand under my chin and lifted my eyes to meet His. "Sharon, you are free from your infirmity of feeling less than. Because of the finished work I did for you on the cross, and because of My spirit in you, you are more than enough to do what I've called you to do and be who I've called you to be."

Not long after that, words began to flow from pen to paper, from paper to pages, from pages to books. You know, I'm sure some onlookers gasped at my courage and glared at my audacity as I stepped out of the shadows. *Who does she think she is?* they might have thought.

And I can answer that question. I am an emotionally bent and bowed woman whom Jesus set straight and let loose. He calls me a child of God, light of the world, salt of the earth, bride of Christ, redeemed, holy, chosen, ambassador, saint...and that's just for starters. And, friend, if you know Jesus Christ as Savior, then that's exactly what He calls you too!

Is there something in your life that is bending your spirit? Unforgiveness? Bitterness? Resentment? Guilt? Sorrow? Worry? Regret? Comparison? If so, cut it loose, cast it off, throw it away. God calls us sheep, and sheep are not pack animals. We are not meant to carry such burdens with these scrawny legs of ours. If we try, we will only bend under pressure we were never meant to bear.

Oh, friend, He is calling you right now. Whatever has been holding you back from lifting your head...Jesus has come to set you straight! Do you feel the press of His hand on the crook of your back? Do you feel His index finger under the point of your chin?

There's no doubt in my mind that you are holding this book because Jesus is calling you from the shadows to join Him center stage. He sees you, and now is the time. You've been sitting in the back, in your crippled state far too long. "Woman, you are set free from your infirmity."

CHAPTER 10

Celebrated

Girl, Your Faith Is Something Else

Belva held her twitching daughter in her arms. With eyes rolled back and thrashing limbs, the child convulsed and then stiffened. "Oh, Mara," the distraught mother cried. "When will this ever end?"

For years little Mara had violently convulsed in predictable synchronized intervals. The child often cried out in a loud, screeching voice, threw herself against the walls of their one-room home, and cut her arms with rocks and broken pottery until blood flowed.

Belva and her daughter lived in Tyre, a Gentile Phoenician city that bordered Galilee along the Mediterranean Sea. Belva was from Canaanite descent—a people who had been enemies of the Jews since they marched into the Promised Land hundreds of years before. The Jews despised the entire region from Tyre to Sidon and avoided it at all costs.

But amid the ungodliness that permeated the city, word of Jesus' miracles and teaching drifted along the streets. Belva drank in the stories. How she longed for a drop of hope to fall on her parched soul. One story caught her attention more than any other.

"Belva, have you heard?" a neighbor began. "Jesus delivered a boy much like your Mara."

"Tell me," Belva asked hungrily. "What happened?"

"A boy in Galilee had an evil spirit that seized him and caused him to scream out for no reason at all. The spirit threw him into convulsions, and he foamed at the mouth. It was destroying the boy—and his father, for that matter."

"Oh, that poor family. What did Jesus do?"

"Well, He was just returning from a trip with three of His disciples. His other disciples had remained back in the village while they were away. This father took his son to them for healing, but the disciples couldn't do a thing for him. But then Jesus and His three friends walked into the crowd, and this father fell at His feet. He begged Jesus to heal his only son. And right as the father was pleading with Jesus, the boy fell to the ground in a convulsion!"

"Oh, my!" Belva clapped her hand over her mouth.

"Then Jesus rebuked the evil spirit. 'Come out of him!' He cried. And just like that, the demon was gone. Jesus picked up the boy and handed him back to his father."

Tears filled Belva's eyes as she listened to this miraculous account. *If only I could go to Jesus. But that was the story of a man and his son. Does God even care about a woman and her little girl? He wouldn't have anything to do with the likes of me, a despised Canaanite woman.*

"Some say He is the Messiah—the Son of David. Who knows? Too bad Jesus won't be coming here," her friend continued. "He would never step foot in this forsaken place."

And with a shrug, Belva's friend walked away.

"Oh, God," Belva prayed later that night, "is there any way You could make an exception for one so lowly as me? I know I am from a cursed race, a despised people, but my daughter is being destroyed. She is only a child. I am not asking for me. I am begging for her. Please send Jesus my way. Please heal my little daughter. You are our only hope." And with those final words on her lips, Belva cried herself to sleep.

"He's here! He's here!" A raucous crowd outside Belva's window startled her from her slumber. She ran to the window and peeked out to see what the commotion was all about. Then she saw Him. No one had to tell her the identity of the stranger walking past her home. She just knew.

"It's Jesus!" she cried.

Belva grabbed her shawl and dashed from her home. Hope was passing by, and she fell at His feet to block the way. "Lord, Son of David, have mercy on me! My little girl suffers from demon possession."

Jesus didn't answer the woman but kept walking along the dusty road.

Again she cried, "Lord, Son of David, please have mercy on me! My daughter is...she is suffering terribly."

"Send this woman away," the disciples urged. "She keeps crying out after us. Get rid of her."

Jesus then paused and spoke to the woman. "I wasn't sent to you, but to the lost sheep of Israel."

Kneeling humbly at His feet, she sobbed. "Lord, help me!"

"It is not right to take bread meant for children and toss it to the dogs," Jesus replied.

"Yes, Lord," she gently whispered, "but even the dogs eat the crumbs that fall from their master's table."

Jesus held out His hand and pulled this woman to her feet—this woman to whom He had been sent. "Woman, you have great faith! Your request is granted."

Belva ran home to find her daughter sitting on her bed, brushing her doll's hair, and in her right mind. She never had another seizure.

Years later, as she often did, Mara asked her mother to tell her a story as she tucked her into bed. "Mommy, tell me the story of Jesus again."

FOR JUST ONE

I love this story on so many levels. I've had to stop and dry my eyes several times before proceeding. Here was a woman that the religious world would have steered clear of, and yet God steered Jesus right to her front door. Let's walk through the details and discover just how much God loves and esteems women—even those (especially those) whom society doesn't believe are worth the ground they walk on.

Jesus withdrew to the region of Tyre and Sidon (Matthew 15:21).

After Jesus' earthly ministry had begun with turning water into wine, He had performed miracles left and right. Just a few days before this encounter with the Syrophoenician woman, He had fed 5,000 men plus women and children with five loaves and two fish. Later that evening, as the disciples struggled to stay afloat in a life-threatening storm on the Sea of Galilee, Jesus defied nature and walked on the water to calm their sinking hearts and the turbulent sea. Even as they sailed away to the distant shore, Jesus knew the religious leaders were behind closed doors plotting to kill Him.

He needed to get away from the hustle and bustle to catch His breath—or at least that's how it appeared to the disciples. But rather than going to a retreat center for a respite, or even to Mary and Martha's for a good meal, Jesus headed to the city of Tyre, some 30 miles away. They traveled on foot for several days over rough and rocky terrain.

Matthew used the word "withdrew." Jesus "withdrew to the region of Tyre and Sidon." He didn't just leave; He withdrew to be by Himself to get away from the crowds.

I am sure the disciples questioned their new itinerary. *If Samaria wasn't bad enough, now we're going to Tyre! That heathen land of the cursed Canaanites! What is He thinking?*

Tyre was a business capital whose position on the coast provided easy access to foreign trade. But along with the bountiful commerce emerged bountiful idol worship. Tyre and Sidon became centers for the worship of Baal and Asherah, where prostitution and human sacrifices were the norm.

Jesus had already said that it was the sick who need a doctor (Matthew 9:12). And this is exactly the sort of place where a doctor would head. Mark tells us, "Jesus left that place and went to the vicinity of Tyre. He entered a house and did not want anyone to know it" (Mark 7:24). But you just can't keep news like that quiet. Jesus was in town!

A Canaanite woman from that vicinity came to him (Matthew 15:22).

Matthew calls her a Canaanite. Apparently he couldn't forget that this gal was from a race of people that were longtime enemies of the Jews. Mark simply refers to her as "a Greek, born in Syrian Phoenicia" (Mark 7:26). Either way, she was a Gentile with "less than" stamped on her forehead.

"Lord, Son of David, have mercy on me! My daughter is demon-possessed and suffering terribly" (Matthew 15:22). Did you notice that not an ounce of pride was in this woman's plea? She didn't care what anyone thought. She was begging for the life of her child. Her greeting hints that she believed Jesus was also God's Son because "Son of David" was a term associated with the coming Messiah.

By approaching a man in public, she was so far out on a limb you can almost hear the branch cracking beneath her feet. But she didn't care. There wasn't anything she wouldn't do for her daughter. She was a gutsy risk taker, and making a public fool of herself was immaterial.

Jesus did not answer a word (Matthew 15:23).

Does it bother you that Jesus didn't answer her right away? Does His silence cause your heart to wince? I'll admit that when I read the words, or lack of them, I find myself cringing a bit. This must have screamed rejection to this wounded woman, but Jesus had something up His sleeve. He was using this as a teaching tool in the lives of the disciples and in the lives of all who would read the words for years to come.

Oh, dear friend, just because we don't hear an immediate response from God does not mean He's not listening. It does not mean He has rejected our request. It may simply mean He has something else in mind or wants to take us to a deeper place of understanding. He may be taking us to a place that is so good, our minds need the pause to find it. What we do see and hear of God's working is miniscule compared to the magnificent workings we cannot see.

> Just because we don't hear an immediate response from God does not mean He's not listening.

Send her away, for she keeps crying out after us (Matthew 15:23).

The disciples hadn't quite grasped Jesus' compassion for the human race. "Be quiet," they scolded the blind man who begged for sight. "Get those kids out of here," they scolded the parents who brought their children to Jesus for a blessing. "Send her away," they encouraged Jesus when this seemingly insignificant mother kept pleading for the life of her child. But she persisted...and God hears the prayers of the persistent. As in Luke's Gospel, Jesus told His disciples a parable to show them that they should always pray and not give up. He said,

> In a certain town there was a judge who neither feared God nor cared what people thought. And there was a widow in

that town who kept coming to him with the plea, "Grant me justice against my adversary." For some time he refused. But finally he said to himself, "Even though I don't fear God or care what people think, yet because this widow keeps bothering me, I will see that she gets justice, so that she won't eventually come and attack me!" (Luke 18:2-5).

In the Gospel of Matthew, He said,

> Keep on asking and it will be given you; seek *and* keep on seeking and you will find; knock and keep on knocking and the door will be opened to you. For everyone who keeps on asking receives, and he who keeps on seeking finds, and to him who keeps on knocking, [the door] will be opened (Matthew 7:7-8 AMP).

Jesus had taught His disciples the principles of persistence in prayer. Now He was taking them on a field trip to see a living example of the spiritual truth. He was going to answer her—after all, that's why He came to town. But not yet...

I was sent only to the lost sheep of Israel (Matthew 15:24).

Well, that is not the answer I was thinking of. Perhaps Jesus was fishing to bring her bold faith to the surface. So He set the bait and waited a moment more.

Matthew tells us the woman knelt before Him, and she cried, "Lord, help me!" (15:25). She had no more words. She didn't know what else to say. Have you ever said those same words? On the days when the waves of emotions swell over us, the undertow of sorrow pulls beneath us, or the fog of confusion settles around us—"Lord, help me!"

I have cried and prayed until there are no more words. God is not impressed with long, flowery prayers. He is impressed, however, with a prayer of faith offered in humility.

It is not right to take the children's bread and toss it to the dogs (Matthew 15:26).

At first glance His words sound demeaning, but in the context of Jesus' life and actions, we know that was never His intent. So we must dig deeper. What was He doing? Why did He respond with such a rebuff? I believe Jesus was teaching—always teaching. He knew her heart before He even saw her face. He wanted the disciples to know it as well.

Gentiles were often called dogs, referring to the disease-ridden scrawny scavengers that roamed the streets, but the Greek word Jesus used here, *kynariois*, is actually more like puppies or domesticated pets. Still, it was not a term of endearment. The woman understood Jesus' implications. She was not one of the sheep the Shepherd had come for, but she didn't let His reference deter her mission. She wasn't offended but acknowledged her lowly state.

Matthew had already recorded stories of Jesus healing a Gentile centurion's servant and delivering two demon-possessed men in the Gentile region of Gadarenes (Matthew 8:5-13, 28-34). Her being a Gentile was not a problem to Jesus. This lets us know that Jesus had a specific motive for His response to the woman. He was fishing for faith.

> "Yes it is, Lord," she said. "Even the dogs eat the crumbs that fall from their master's table" (Matthew 15:27).

Bingo. There it is. Once again, Jesus used the woman's words to teach about the power of faith. As if He were saying, "Watch this, boys," Jesus goads her to reveal what real faith looks like. Like many times before, Jesus called a woman center stage for a teaching moment for us all. I believe Jesus smiled at her words. He answered, "Woman, you have great faith! Your request is granted" (Matthew 15:28).

I love how Eugene Peterson paraphrases Jesus' comments to our Syrophoenician sister: "'Oh, woman, your faith is something else. What you want is what you get!' Right then her daughter became well" (MSG).

Only two people in the Gospel of Matthew are commended for their great faith: the centurion who asked Jesus to heal his servant recorded in Matthew 8:10 and this Canaanite woman in Tyre who begged for the health of her daughter. Both came to Jesus on behalf of someone they loved dearly. Both were Gentiles who believed in the Jewish Messiah who came for all.

THAT'S A WRAP

Now here's the clincher to the entire story. After this encounter, "Jesus left there and went along the Sea of Galilee" (Matthew 15:29). This mission was complete. The Syrophoenician mother was His sole assignment for the entire journey. We don't hear about any other teachings or healings. Why so much trouble for one woman? Because she was worth it. Would Jesus go through all that trouble for one woman and her little girl? You bet He would! That's how significant God's daughters are to Him.

Just as Jesus "had to go to Samaria," I believe He had to go to Tyre. A woman who needed Him lived there. A woman who had cried out to God for the life of her child. And on God's kingdom calendar, written on Jesus' celestial planner, her name appeared.

In the story of Jesus and the Syrophoenician mother, we see Jesus once again going out of His way to minister to a desperate, seemingly insignificant woman. This trend must have been cause for pause among the disciples. It certainly wasn't what they expected. Jesus consistently elevated women to heights of significance and dignity that ran contrary to all they had ever known. Jesus loves shattering race, rank, and religious barriers to call women center stage. He did it then. He does it now.

We don't know her name. I've simply put a name with the story so we can picture her in our mind's eye. But here's the thing: Jesus knew her name. Jesus knew her address. Jesus knew her need. And sister,

He knows your name, your address, and your need as well. No matter what you may think of yourself, Jesus thinks you are worth the trip!

Jesus loves shattering race, rank, and religious barriers to call women center stage. He did it then. He does it now.

CHAPTER 11

Admired

Making Much of Little

Beatrice woke as the morning sun peeked through the shutters of her sparse bedroom. Every joint in her old body creaked like a grinding wheel in dire need of good oiling. Her arthritic hands rubbed sleepy eyes, and then she instinctively reached to the empty space where her husband slept so many years ago.

"Another Sabbath to worship Jehovah," she smiled. "Lord, thank You for the health and strength to travel to Your house today. Thank You for the many blessings You have showered on this old woman."

Beatrice slipped on her worn woolen garment, wound her wispy gray hair around her head, and splashed yesterday's water on her wrinkled face. She retrieved her money pouch from its hiding place behind a group of jars and slipped her hand inside, fumbling to gather an offering for the temple coffers.

A sigh escaped her lips as she retrieved only two small coins. She reached back into the pouch and ran her fingers from side to side. This time she came up empty.

Looking at the coins in her hand, she continued her conversation with God. "I wish I had more to give You today, but Lord, this is all I have." Not once did Beatrice wonder how she would buy grain for her next meal. She knew God would provide. He always did.

Beatrice shuffled out the door and through the busy streets of Jerusalem. The population had more than doubled because of the Passover celebration. Jews from miles around gathered at the temple during the holy week.

People, people, everywhere people, Beatrice thought. *And not one notices an old worthless widow like me.* She kept her eyes down as she climbed the first set of steps to the women's court in the temple. *I'm glad I'm not a man or priest. I don't think I could climb all those stairs to get to the upper levels.*

The widow made her way to the same offering receptacle she always used. When she raised her eyes to place the two small coins in the container, she noticed a man sitting beside it as though waiting for someone. Color rose to her cheeks as she realized it was Jesus, and that He was watching her. Beatrice cringed with embarrassment as she dropped her two small coins into the large box. *What must He think of me? Only two copper coins.*

When she looked up and met Jesus' gaze, He grinned from ear to ear and nodded His approval. Every wrinkle in her face crinkled as she returned the smile. But what He said next almost made her feel like a spry young girl again.

"Peter, John, James. Friends, come over here," Jesus called. "You're looking around at all these people dropping their coins in the temple treasury, and I'm sure you have noticed that some of the wealthy made large donations. At least, they are hoping you've noticed. But I tell you the truth, this poor widow has put more in the treasury than all the others. They all gave out of their wealth. That was no sacrifice at all. It was just surplus. But this woman gave out of her poverty." Jesus placed His hand on Beatrice's shoulder. "She gave all she had to live on. Her gift is more precious to God than all the others combined."

Beatrice bowed and turned to leave. Jesus laughed to Himself, thinking about what she would find in her money pouch when she got home.

MAKING MUCH OF LITTLE

This is the last recorded incident in Jesus' public ministry before He made His final preparations for the cross. All the way from Galilee to Jerusalem, He had been teaching the disciples about the high cost of discipleship. "Those who humble themselves will be exalted" (Luke 14:11). "Whoever does not carry their cross and follow me cannot be my disciple" (Luke 14:27). "In the same way, those of you who do not give up everything you have cannot be my disciples" (Luke 14:33). Now, as they arrived at the temple in Jerusalem, Jesus showed them a practical example of His spiritual teaching.

This was Passover week, and Jerusalem was teeming with Jews participating in the festivities. Jesus had been teaching for the better part of the day, knowing this would be His last chance to speak to the multitudes in the temple. After teaching, He moved to where the offerings were placed to teach His disciples about true giving.

Remember, during the time of Jesus, Herod's Temple was partitioned off in various segments allowing only certain types of people in each area. Each partition was separated by a set of steps that led up to the next one. Higher and higher the Jewish leaders elevated themselves from the rest of the common folks. Gentiles at the bottom, then Jewish women, then Jewish men, then priests, then the high priest.

I want you to keep that picture in mind. Let's walk up the steps from the court of Gentiles and join Jesus in the court of women.

> Jesus sat down opposite the place where the offerings were put and watched the crowd putting their money into the temple treasury (Mark 12:41).

The temple treasury was located in the court of women on the second level. This is where all worshippers gave their tithes and offerings. Thirteen boxes, shaped like inverted megaphones or trumpets, lined the walls to receive the money. In this particular story, it was Passover week, so a steady flow of pilgrims deposited their contributions.

Jesus, the Creator of the universe, the God-made man, the Great High Priest, didn't go past gate two, gate three, gate four, or gate five. Rather, He stayed in the women's court with the common folk—with His people. But there was one woman in particular He was waiting for. He knew she was coming. He was expecting her.

Picture Jesus pulling up a chair by a certain offering box, knowing exactly which one the widow would be coming to. He was waiting for her; she just didn't know it.

One by one, wealthy attendees tossed their coins into the coffers. I can almost hear the clanging now. The more noise the offering made, the better. "Look at me! Look at me!" the loud clanging coins announced. "I'm giving a lot today. Why? Because I'm important. I'm wealthy. I'm holy. Don't you wish you could be more like me?"

But then, here she came. A shabbily dressed, worn-down old woman. She timidly approached the offering box and gingerly placed her treasure among the coins. The others "threw." She "put." Two small copper coins—the smallest coins in circulation in Palestine—just a fraction of a penny. Two of these lepton, as they were called, were worth a sixty-fourth of a denarius, a typical day's wage. But in reality, her coins were worth more than any day's wages. They were all she had—and Jesus knew it.

Do you ever feel that other people don't really care about what is going on in your life? Do you feel insignificant in the grand scheme of things? I am sure this widow must have felt less than. *I'm nothing. I have nothing. I am invisible to these men with flowing robes and tasseled garb.*

Ever been there? I have. But she wasn't insignificant or less than. Jesus was waiting for her arrival—for her gift. "For the eyes of the LORD range throughout the earth to strengthen those whose hearts are fully committed to him" (2 Chronicles 16:9).

> Calling his disciples to him, Jesus said, "Truly I tell you, this poor widow has put more into the treasury than all the others. They all gave out of their wealth; but she, out of her poverty, put in everything—all she had to live on" (Mark 12:43-44).

Jesus was waiting for this widow. He knew she was coming. And He used this seemingly insignificant woman to teach His disciples about significant giving.

The widow only had two copper coins. I wonder what I would have done in the same situation. I think I would have been tempted to just give one to the temple treasury and keep one for myself. *One for You. One for me. After all, God wouldn't want me to go hungry, would He?*

The widow did not give one coin and keep one for herself. She gave all she had, fully trusting that God would take care of her every need. Commentators have pointed out that when Jesus said, "She out of her poverty put in all she had to live on" (Luke 21:4), the phrase "to live on" is the Greek word *bios*, which means she gave her *life* itself.

LOOK AND LEARN

One summer my family and I traveled to Yellowstone Park and Jackson Hole, Wyoming. One of our goals was to see as many unusual animals as possible. For us that was anything other than a dog, cat, or bird. During the entire trip, we were on the lookout for moose, elk, buffalo, and other furry beasts with antlers. After several days we fell into the rhythm of looking for groupings of cars stopped alongside the road or crowds clustered in the woods. This signaled a sighting! As if holding up a neon sign, the assembly let us know we needed to stop. There was some magnificent creature we needed to see.

That's what I see happening in the temple the day the widow gave all she had. Jesus calls the disciples over to see the widow and her gift. Thirteen men gather round the offering box as Jesus shines the spotlight on this woman's sacrificial act. Now, what else do you see? I see other people migrating to the scene. "What's so important?" they ask. "What's going on?" "What are you men looking at?" Then Jesus lifts His hand and directs their attention to one of God's magnificent creations. Ta-da! She simply nods, smiles, and walks away.

I don't think for a minute Jesus let her walk away and live the rest of her life empty-handed. I would love to know what happened to her as the days and weeks followed her sacrificial gift. Jesus gives us a hint in His other teachings.

"Give, and it will be given to you. A good measure, pressed down, shaken together and running over, will be poured into your lap. For with the measure you use, it will be measured to you" (Luke 6:38). In those days, men and women wore robes that were held together with belts. Extra fabric bloused out over the belt that served as a large pocket. Wearers used this large pocket to carry wheat. So when Jesus said blessings would be poured into your lap, He was giving the picture of sustenance filling up and overflowing their pockets.

What is done in secret never goes unnoticed by God. "Your Father, who sees what is done in secret, will reward you" (Matthew 6:18). "Whoever sows generously will also reap generously" (2 Corinthians 9:6).

How precious that Jesus used the gift of a seemingly insignificant woman to teach the disciples about significant giving. She became a "look and learn" example to this burly bunch of men—and to you and me.

Jesus took His spotlight and shone it on one widowed woman to show us a picture of significant sacrifice. While she might have felt worthless in the world's eyes, she was priceless to God. She was the star of her scene and played the leading role in this near-final segment of Jesus' story.

 Commissioned

Go and Tell

She was just a normal little girl frolicking about the house, playing with their goats and sticking her fingers in her mother's rising dough. After her father died, Mary watched her mother try her best to raise her on what little money he'd left behind. But when puberty began to bloom, a poisonous weed took root in her mind. With each passing year, her behavior grew more and more erratic.

Often she was seen banging her head against the wall of their modest home, screaming curses to unseen shadows, crawling like an animal through the yard, and cutting her arms with sharp-edged stones. Mary's mother was almost relieved when the deranged young woman ran away to live among the tombs.

Mary Magdalene was a demon-possessed lunatic—unwanted, unclean, untouchable, and unapproachable. She was less than the least. But that was about to change.

"Peter," Jesus said as He led the group of men toward the cemetery on the fringes of Magdala. "I need to stop here for a moment."

"But why?" John questioned. "Do you have a relative's grave you wish to visit?"

"Not a physically dead relative, but a spiritually dead sister who needs me."

With confusion on their faces, the disciples knew not to argue with Jesus' travel plans. It seemed He always had a purpose in mind.

As soon as the Twelve neared the tombs, a half-dressed woman in tattered rags bolted from the brush.

"We know who You are," the woman hissed. "You are the Son of God. What do You want with us?"

The disciples recoiled at the sight and stench of this madwoman, but Jesus drew near. Certainly, this was not the sister He mentioned. With a shout, Jesus directed His words *toward* the woman but rebuked the demons *in* the woman. "Come out of her!"

The woman fell to the ground in a violent seizure. After a few moments of bloodcurdling screams and obscene curses, she lay perfectly still.

"Is she dead?" James asked.

"No," Jesus replied. "She is actually more alive than she's ever been."

Jesus knelt down beside her, brushed the hair from her eyes, and extended His hand. "Mary, rise up and live free."

The disciples stared wide-eyed as Mary rose to her feet, finally in her right mind. Her crazed countenance was replaced by calm composure.

"Thank you, thank you," she cried as tears of freedom and joy coursed down her dusty cheeks.

Jesus turned to walk away to His next assignment, but rather than stand and stare in awe, Mary ran to follow. The disciples waited for Jesus to send her away. They were quite surprised when He did just the opposite and motioned for her to come along. From that day on, she would remain among the disciples to do whatever she could to further the ministry of Jesus.

DELIVERED

We don't know much about Mary Magdalene's encounter with Jesus and her deliverance from demons. A closer look at her emancipation only allows us to examine one solitary sentence. "The Twelve were with him, and also some women who had been cured of evil spirits and diseases: Mary (called Magdalene) from whom seven demons had come out" (Luke 8:1-2).

Even though we don't know much about what Mary was like before her encounter with Jesus, the Bible gives us many snapshots of men and women possessed by demons. They threw themselves into fire (Matthew 17:15), thrashed on the ground (Luke 4:35), violently convulsed (Matthew 17:15), cried out (Mark 5:5; Luke 4:33-34; 8:28), exhibited unrestrainable superhuman strength (Luke 8:29; Mark 5:4), and foamed at the mouth (Luke 9:39). Some cut themselves with sharp objects (Mark 5:5), while others ran about naked and lived among the tombs (Luke 8:27). Some were blind (Matthew 12:22) and others mute (Matthew 12:22; Luke 11:14). While we don't know the exact manifestations Mary Magdalene exhibited, we can assume she lived a dark and deranged existence controlled by demons that haunted her day and night. Let's take a closer look at Mary to glean from the few verses we *do* have.

After this, Jesus traveled about from one town and village to another (Luke 8:1).

After what? That's a good question. Since Jesus' time of ministry had begun, He had been baptized by His cousin John in the Jordan River, tempted by His enemy Satan in the wilderness, and empowered by the Holy Spirit to perform miracles in urban centers and small villages alike. Jesus had chosen His 12 key disciples, raised a widow's son from the dead, and taught the multitudes.

Jesus continued His travels proclaiming the gospel—the good news of grace, repentance, forgiveness of sins, and the promise of eternal life.

He explained new spiritual truths with everyday stories people could understand. And while He taught anyone who would listen, a handful of people also traveled with Him from place to place.

> The Twelve were with him, and also some women who had been cured of evil spirits and diseases: Mary (called Magdalene) from whom seven demons had come out; Joanna the wife of Chuza, the manager of Herod's household; Susanna; and many others (Luke 8:1-3).

For most of my life I pictured Jesus traveling about with His 12 disciples. After all, isn't that the picture in the Sunday school books? It was only as an adult that the landscape in my mind changed dramatically. I had to walk over to the easel and paint a new picture on a fresh canvas. Jesus didn't travel about with only the 12 men. Luke lets us know that there were women who traveled with them as well: Mary Magdalene, Joanna, Susanna, and many others.

And many others. I just love that. These were women who had been healed, delivered, saved, and empowered by Jesus. Where had they been all my life? They had been there all along, but somehow, I missed their influence on Jesus' earthly ministry until I began to dig deeper and see what the Bible really said. I had allowed ancient artists to paint the pictures of Jesus and His entourage in my mind rather than Scripture. Unfortunately, for many years, art was "the Bible for the illiterate"[1] and the cause of many myths of Mary Magdalene being passed down through the centuries. Aren't you glad we live in a day when we can hold a Bible in our hands and learn God's truth directly from Him?

DISCIPLED

So who was Mary Magdalene? Of all the women in the Bible, perhaps she is surrounded with the most mystery, presumption, and speculation. We're not given a lot of information except where she was from and what she had been like before she met Jesus.

Eight out of nine times in the Bible when Mary Magdalene is mentioned with a grouping of other women, her name appears first. In that culture, "the order of naming indicated the order of importance."[2] More than 50 percent of the women in Palestine in Jesus' day were named either Mary or Salome.[3] That's a lot of Marys—we've looked at three! It's understandable that they have been confused. But Mary Magdalene "was clearly a woman of prominence, not to be confused with any other Mary in the New Testament. Everybody knew which woman you were talking about when you said, 'Mary Magdalene.'"[4]

We also know that Mary was from Magdala, one of nine cities on the western shore of the Sea of Galilee.[5] It stood along the ancient road from Nazareth to Damascus, not far south of Capernaum.[6] Though its name doesn't appear on modern-day maps, Magdala was in the heartland of Jesus' ministry.

Throughout history, Mary Magdalene's identity has been confused with other women in the New Testament. Some have suggested that she was the sinful woman who anointed Jesus' feet at the Pharisee's dinner party (Luke 7:37-38). But Luke tells the story of the woman anointing Jesus' feet in chapter 7 and then introduces Mary Magdalene for the first time in chapter 8. Nowhere is Mary Magdalene ever mentioned as a "sinful woman." She was simply a woman from whom Jesus cast seven demons. These are two entirely different women, regardless of what the Renaissance painters have portrayed.

Some have even suggested that Mary Magdalene was the woman caught in adultery. But I don't know of many men who would be drawn to a woman possessed by seven demons, especially from what we've learned about the typical manifestations of other demoniacs. Not once in the New Testament do we read of Jesus delivering someone from demons and then saying, "Your sins are forgiven." Nowhere does

Jesus use the word *sinful* to describe someone possessed by demons. Another clue that these two women are not one and the same is found in Jesus' final words to the woman caught in adultery. His final charge was "go in peace" (Luke 7:50), not "come follow Me."

Here's what we know: Mary Magdalene was a woman possessed and controlled by seven demons, but at some point she had an encounter with Jesus, who delivered her from the clutches of Satan and into the hands of God. From that point on, I believe Mary's mission in life was to do what she could to serve her Savior, Lord, Healer, Redeemer, and Teacher. And how did she do that? Luke 8:3 tells us, "These women were helping to support them out of their own means."

Like most women, I sense that Mary and the other women did what needed doing. They saw a need and met it. They supported Jesus and His ministry financially, personally, and spiritually. The word "helping" is from the Greek word *diaokinos*, which is sometimes translated "minister." It is where we get the word *deacon* or *deaconess*.

"Out of their own means" has also been translated "considerable means" (MSG), "private means" (NASB), and "their own resources" (NET). We aren't told where these women obtained their sizable nest eggs, but we know they were generous women of means.

These women also sat at Jesus' feet as He taught, ignoring cultural and religious man-made boundaries that prohibited women from sitting under the teaching of a rabbi. When Mary Magdalene met the resurrected Jesus at the empty garden tomb, she addressed Him as "Teacher." She didn't call Him "Healer," "Provider," or "Ruler." Jesus is indeed all that and more, but her first instinct was to address Him in the way she knew best; He was her teacher who discipled her.

It seems these women were just as willing to go against the social norms to serve Jesus as Jesus was willing to cross gender boundaries to invite them. I'm so glad they said yes. And as for Mary Magdalene, her most important assignment was yet to come.

ON THE THIRD DAY

In a matter of three years, Jesus had turned the world upside down. His followers had great expectations for how His earthly reign would play out. And even though Jesus had tried to prepare them, they were taken completely off guard by His arrest and crucifixion. When His body was sealed away in that darkened tomb, their hopes and dreams were sealed away as well. Mary was among those whose shattered dreams lay scattered under the cross. Little did she know that the best was yet to come. Let's join her in the wee hours on that Sunday morning so many years ago.

It was still dark as Mary arose from yet another sleepless night of tossing and turning. The horrific events of Friday's crucifixion played over and over in her mind. Her hopes and dreams drained out with every drop of Jesus' blood. When He uttered the words, "It is finished," she felt that her life was finished as well.

Mary had pinned all her hopes and dreams on Jesus. He had given her a new mind, a new purpose, and a new life. But now that He was gone, the chains of the past rattled in the background. Fear was knocking at the door. Would she get sick again? Would the demons return? What would she do?

"I can't believe this happened," she cried to herself as she paced the cold, hard floor. "What am I going to do without Him?" But suddenly, Mary knew what she had to do. An unexplainable urge led her to the box of spices on the kitchen shelf and then out the door. "I must go to Him," she whispered. She gathered Joanna, Salome, and Mary the mother of James, and the foursome made their way to the tomb before the first stream of sunlight streaked the sky.

A predawn mist hovered over the garden surrounding the tomb where Jesus' body had been laid days earlier. "Mary," Salome asked, "who will roll the stone away from the entrance so we can attend to Jesus' body?"

"I don't know, Salome. We'll worry about that when we get there."

Broken and shattered, the women moved in deep sorrow and mourning over the death of their beloved Savior and Lord. *Why?* Mary silently cried. *Why did God allow this to happen?*

As the women approached the tomb, something was amiss. No guards and, more importantly, no stone. Mary ran to the entrance of the open tomb and peered inside to find it empty. She crumpled to the ground in a heap. "Who would have done such a thing? Isn't it enough that they tortured, beat, and crucified this innocent man? Why would they have stolen His body too?" The other women cried in a huddle, clinging to one another with questions.

"I must go and tell the others," Mary said as she dried her tears and dashed from the empty tomb. Off she ran to where the disciples were still hiding.

"They took Him!" Mary cried as she burst through the door. "His body is gone!"

Without asking any questions, Peter jumped up from the table and bolted from the room. The much younger and more agile John followed close behind, eventually passing his older friend.

"He's not here," John whispered as he peered inside the opening of the cave. "His body is gone." A moment later, a breathless Peter arrived. He didn't stop at the mouth of the cave but rushed in Peter-style. "Look," John said to his winded friend. "Over there in the corner."

A ray of sunlight pierced the darkness and pointed their attention to Jesus' empty burial cloths. Strips of linen that had once covered Jesus' head now lay folded neatly in a corner like a carpenter's cloths after a finished job.

"What happened here? What does this mean?" they asked one another.

Peter and John went back to report their findings to the other disciples, while Mary Magdalene stayed behind. Deep guttural cries of mourning filled the quiet as she knelt by the empty tomb. Suddenly, a beam of light caught her attention. There, at the spot where Jesus' body had been laid, sat two glistening angels clothed in white.

"Woman, why are you crying?" one of the angels asked.

"They have taken my Master," Mary replied through her tears. "I don't know where they have taken Him."

Hearing a rustling in the myrtle bushes behind her, Mary turned her head. She felt a presence and discerned she was not alone. Someone was in the garden with her.

"Woman, why are you weeping?" the man asked.

Thinking the man was the gardener, she cried, "Sir, if you know where they have taken Jesus, would you please tell me so I can take care of Him?"

Then Jesus said one simple word: "Mary."

At the sound of her name, Mary recognized the risen Lord.

"Rabboni!" she cried. The One who had taught her, who had instructed her, who had loved her was alive!

Mary fell on her knees and clung to Jesus' feet with a blending of tears and laughter. There was so much she wanted to say, to ask. But her words were lost in emotion.

"You have to let me go," Jesus said softly, "for I haven't yet returned to My Father. Please go to My brothers and tell them I am alive." With a smile that put the rising sun to shame, Mary turned and ran to tell the others the good news. Jesus had risen, just like He said.

"I have seen Him! I have seen the Lord!"

SINGLED OUT AND SENT OUT

Jesus knew it was coming. He tried to warn the disciples. Death loomed in the air with swirls of bloodthirsty hatred circling the Son of God. But somehow the disciples didn't understand the imminence of Jesus' crucifixion, and they certainly didn't comprehend the promise of His resurrection. Mary Magdalene didn't understand it either. However, she was there until the end…and at the new beginning for us all.

After Jesus' arrest, His 11 surprised disciples scattered like church mice when the lights come on. But not Mary Magdalene. She watched in horror as His beaten body was stripped naked, nailed to the cruel Roman cross, and displayed before a gawking crowd. She stood close by as His precious blood dripped from His thorn-pierced brow and onto the cursed ground. Mary watched closely when His lifeless body was lowered from the cross, and she followed quietly when they laid Him in the borrowed tomb. We get no stories of Mary Magdalene running away from the authorities, hiding behind locked doors, or denying her association with Jesus from curious bystanders. Is it any wonder that Jesus chose this loyal disciple to be the first one to see His resurrected form?

Jesus' resurrection was the most pivotal point in all of history, and yet He waited until Peter and John had left the empty tomb before making His presence known to one lone woman. Jesus was standing center stage, and He extended His hand for Mary Magdalene to join Him front and center. Let's go back to the Scripture and take a closer look at the most important event in human history.

> Near the cross of Jesus stood his mother, his mother's sister, Mary the wife of Clopas, and Mary Magdalene (John 19:25).

While most of the disciples scattered in fear at the arrest and crucifixion of Jesus, Mary Magdalene, along with some of the other leading women, stood at the cross until the end. They heard the low moans of His suffering, watched the streams of blood splatter the ground, and saw the last beat of His broken heart.

As the crowd of observers and mourners parted the scene, two remained: Mary, the mother of James and Joseph, and Mary Magdalene. They were there when two men, Joseph of Arimathea and Nicodemus, took Jesus' body down from the cross, prepared Him for burial, and placed Him in the garden tomb.

Who will roll the stone away from the entrance of the tomb? (Mark 16:3).

The women "worried out loud to each other" (MSG) about how they were going to move the stone away from the opening of the cave. This was no small task. The burial chamber was "sealed with a cut, disk-shaped stone that rolled in a slot cut into the rock. The slot was on an incline, making the grave easy to seal but difficult to open: several men might be needed to roll the stone back."[7]

> But when they looked up, they saw that the stone, which was very large, had been rolled away. As they entered the tomb, they saw a young man dressed in a white robe sitting on the right side, and they were alarmed. "Don't be alarmed," he said. "You are looking for Jesus the Nazarene, who was crucified. He has risen! He is not here. See the place where they laid him. But go, tell his disciples and Peter, 'He is going ahead of you into Galilee. There you will see him, just as he told you'" (Mark 16:4-7).

John tells us more about what happened next. The women did indeed tell the disciples what they saw. Matthew tells us that they "hurried away from the tomb, afraid yet filled with joy" (Matthew 28:8). I can see our sisters now, laughing and crying, relieved and apprehensive, certain and confused. Finally, they reached the men and shouted the news!

Peter and John rushed back to the tomb and found it just as the women had testified—empty. John tells us he "saw and believed" (John

20:8). However, the sentence lacks a direct object, which means it doesn't tell us *what* he believed. The next sentence gives us a clue. "They still did not understand from Scripture that Jesus had to rise from the dead" (John 20:9). Mark records: "They did not believe it" (16:11). Luke wrote, "But they did not believe the women, because their words seemed to them like nonsense" (24:11). So what did John believe? He believed that the tomb was empty. Theologian Matthew Henry wrote: "One cannot but be amazed at the stupidity of these disciples."[8] (I didn't say it. Mr. Henry did.)

Well, Peter and John "went back to where they were staying" (John 20:10). This is further proof the disciples didn't believe Mary's report that Jesus had risen from the dead. If they had believed her, they would have been celebrating and looking for Him rather than slinking back home in defeat.

Mary stood outside the tomb crying (John 20:11).

"As she wept, she bent over to look into the tomb and saw two angels in white, seated where Jesus' body had been, one at the head and the other at the foot" (John 20:11-12). The two angels were in the very same position as the angels on the Ark of the Covenant—one at the head and one at the foot. I wonder if Mary drew the parallel between the Ark of the Covenant, which was a shadow of the reality she was seeing this very day. And while the angels sat before her, it was another voice behind her that changed everything.

> He asked her, "Woman, why are you crying? Who it is you are looking for?" Thinking he was the gardener, she said, "Sir, if you have carried him away, tell me where you have put him, and I will get him." Jesus said to her, "Mary" (John 20:15-16).

My heart just skips a beat every time I read these words. I see myself weeping with Mary as she is down on her knees with gut-wrenching sorrow. All of her dreams were shattered. The empty tomb had erased the most important three years of her life. But then...

As soon as He said her name, Mary knew it was Jesus.

Earlier Jesus had taught, "I am the good shepherd; I know my sheep and my sheep know me...My sheep listen to my voice; I know them, and they follow me" (John 10:14,27). When the Shepherd spoke her name, this precious lamb recognized Him right away.

And what was the first word the risen Savior spoke? "Woman." Don't you love it! Jesus came to set women free from societal, cultural, and religious oppression. He honored women. He respected women. He appointed women. His first spoken word after His resurrection was directed to one of us—and in a sense it was meant for *all* of us—woman.

> She turned toward him and cried out in Aramaic, "Rabboni!" (which means "Teacher"). Jesus said, "Do not hold on to me, for I have not yet ascended to the Father. Go instead to my brothers and tell them, 'I am ascending to my Father and your Father, to my God and your God'" (John 20:16-17).

What did Mary do when she realized Jesus was alive? The same thing I would do if I realized that someone I loved who was presumed dead suddenly appeared. I'd grab that person and hang on for dear life! The Greek word for "hold on to me" actually means "to clutch or grip." One version translates the word as "stop clinging to Me" (NASB). As Liz Curtis Higgs puts it, "Not only did she need to release her grip on his clothing, she also needed to let go of her old definition of who Jesus was. Her friend and teacher had suddenly become a great deal more than a righteous man rooted to her time and place. He was now a risen Savior for all mankind, for all time."[9]

Mary needed to let go of Jesus because He was sending her on a special assignment. He commissioned her with the most important message in all human history: Jesus was alive. Just as God chose

Mary of Bethlehem to bring the baby Jesus into the world, so God commissioned Mary of Magdala to bring news of the risen Christ to the world.

*Mary Magdalene went to the disciples with the news
(John 20:18).*

All four Gospels agree that Mary was the first to witness the resurrection and the first to tell the news. Peter and John were two of Jesus' closest friends. In his Gospel, John refers to himself as "the one Jesus loved" (John 20:2). And yet, when Peter and John arrived at the empty tomb, Jesus kept quiet. He waited until they had gone, and Mary Magdalene was alone.

Why? I don't know all the reasons why He did it. I just know that He did. During a time in history when women were considered on the lowest rung of the social ladder, and their testimony was considered so worthless they weren't even allowed to serve as witnesses in the Jewish court of law, God handpicked Mary Magdalene to be the primary eyewitness to the most significant event in all of history. Then He commissioned her to go and tell about it. For this reason, Mary is often referred to as "the disciple to the disciples," or as Augustine described her, "the apostle of the apostles."

Another remarkable fact about a woman being the chief witness to the empty tomb is that it actually authenticates the account. If someone were to make it up, they surely would have had Jesus' male friends make the discovery. The fact that all four accounts of the gospel have the women being the first to discover the empty tomb shows how faithful the writers were to the facts, regardless of how embarrassing it may have been to them.

Interestingly, "Magdala" is from the Hebrew word *migdol*, which means "a tower or watchtower." How beautifully those words describe our beloved sister, for she was truly the watchtower who first spotted the resurrected Jesus and shouted the news to anyone who would listen.

CALLED AND COMMISSIONED

While most of us have probably not experienced spiritual darkness to the extent of our sister Mary Magdalene, we have all lived it to some degree. The Bible tells us that before we come to Christ, we live in darkness (1 Peter 2:9). Not only were we *in* darkness; we *were* darkness. Paul wrote, "For you were once darkness, but now you are light in the Lord" (Ephesians 5:8).

Like Mary Magdalene, we have been set free from spiritual darkness. "He [the Father] has rescued us from the dominion of darkness and brought us into the kingdom of the Son he loves" (Colossians 1:13). We have more in common with our sister Mary Magdalene than we might have originally thought.

In most cases, men and women with physical illnesses came to Jesus for healing. They traveled miles, bore holes through rooftops, grabbed at His clothes, and fell pleading at His feet. But when it came to those possessed by demons, Jesus went to them or a relative came begging for help. We can safely assume that Jesus went to Mary Magdalene. One day, she was Jesus' assignment. I love how Eugene Peterson paraphrases Ephesians 1:11-12: "Long before we first heard of Christ...he had his eye on us, had designs on us for glorious living, part of the overall purpose he is working out in everything and everyone" (MSG).

God had a plan for Mary Magdalene, and the enemy couldn't stop it no matter how hard he tried. She wasn't seeking Him, but "Jesus' strong arm reached into the black darkness that engulfed her and pulled her out to safety anyway."[10] He set her free from spiritual darkness, restored her dignity, and gave her a place in His personal ministry team. Mary Magdalene is a breathtaking example that our past does not determine our future.

Regardless of all the supposition surrounding the name of Mary Magdalene, the facts show that she was one of the most significant women in the New Testament. She enjoyed a personal, ongoing relationship with Jesus. While most women had an encounter with Jesus that changed their lives, Mary had an encounter plus a face-to-face relationship that continued beyond His death and resurrection to the Father.

Could it be that Jesus was teaching the disciples the value of women's input during this time when females had been secluded and excluded from anything of religious merit? The new order called the church was to be a blending of male and female image bearers working together to spread the gospel and build the body of Christ. Jesus was showing them how.

Jesus ignored cultural norms that treated women as second-class, low-life creatures who were less than their male counterparts. Women who had been previously kept sequestered in their homes now struck out on a radical mission to change the world. Jesus broke the chains that had women bound. This carpenter from Nazareth demolished culturally built walls and constructed doorways for women to walk through. He gave them expanded roles in ministry and validated them as leaders. Jesus called women out from being mere stagehands and onto center stage to assume leading roles.

On that first Easter morning, when God rolled away the stone, it was not just to let Jesus out, but to let the women in. He still rolls away the stones to allow us to enter places we never dreamed possible, to go beyond barriers we never thought crossable, and to minister to people we never imagined reachable.

> Mary Magdalene is a breathtaking example
> that our past does not determine our future.

I hope you are seeing yourself through Jesus' eyes. I hope you are catching a glimpse of your potential to impact your part of the world with the gospel. I hope you are getting a taste of the incredible significance you have as an ambassador to go and tell.

PART 3

Curtain Call

CHAPTER 13

Writing Your Name in the Story

Oh these women! They have taken my breath away with their bodacious courage. And the hero of the story, Jesus, has made my heart swell with knowing just how much He loves us…God's daughters. Created as image bearers. Grafted in as daughters of Abraham. Transformed into coheirs with Christ.

And now it's time for the curtain call—a final look at the female characters of the greatest story ever told and its main character…Jesus. On the stage, a curtain call occurs at the end of a performance when the performers return to the stage to be recognized by the audience. In film, the curtain call is a sequence of short clips, stills, or outtakes featuring the main characters. So let's do just that. Let's take one more look at the characters as a whole, like pieces of a puzzle that have now been completed.

PUTTING THE PUZZLE
PIECES TOGETHER

Let's go back to where we started in chapter 1. During one of Philip's last conversations with Jesus, he asked, "Lord, show us the Father and that will be enough for us" (John 14:8).

Seemingly frustrated, Jesus answered: "Don't you know me, Philip, even after I have been among you such a long time? Anyone who has seen me has seen the Father. How can you say, 'Show us the Father'? Don't you believe that I am in the Father, and that the Father is in me? The words I say to you I do not speak on my own authority. Rather, it is the Father, living in me, who is doing his work. Believe me when I say that I am in the Father and the Father is in me; or at least believe on the evidence of the works themselves" (John 14:9-11).

The writer of Hebrews tells us that Jesus is "the exact representation of [God's] being" (Hebrews 1:3). The original Greek word for "exact representation," *charakter*, describes the impress of a die or the impression of a coin. For example, if you took a coin and pressed it into wax, you would have an exact representation. So when we see Jesus, we see God.

On their way home from celebrating the Passover, Mary and Joseph noticed that their 12-year-old was missing from the caravan. After a three-day search, they found Jesus sitting among the teachers of the temple, listening and asking questions. When Mary questioned Him about why He stayed behind, Jesus responded, "I must be about my Father's business" (Luke 2:49 KJV). Twenty-one years later Jesus breathed His last with the words, "It is finished" (John 19:30). In the years sandwiched between these two statements, Jesus went about His Father's business of restoring mankind, including the women who had felt less than for hundreds of years.

Jesus' attitude and actions toward women were in stark contrast to the religious leaders of His day. While the Pharisees avoided women, Jesus associated freely and spoke openly with them.

- He touched the unclean woman with the flow of blood.

- He taught the hungry female pupil in a room full of men.

- He encouraged Martha to join the classroom.

- He befriended the sisters of Bethany.

- He conversed with the thirsty Samaritan by the well.

- He revealed His true identity to the five-time divorcée.

- He welcomed the sinful woman's worship.

- He called the woman with the crippled back from the shadows.

- He invited Mary Magdalene to join His ministry team.

- He defended Mary of Bethany's gesture when she anointed Him with perfume.

- He commended the Syrophoenician mother's faith.

- He applauded the widow's offering.

- He commissioned Mary Magdalene to go and tell the disciples of His resurrection.

He taught in places where women would be present: on a hillside, along the streets, in the marketplace, by a river, beside a well, and in the women's area of the temple. His longest recorded conversation in the New Testament was with a woman. And as we saw through the lives of several of the women in the New Testament, some of His best students and most daring disciples were women.

And what was Jesus' first word after His resurrection? "Woman."

Jesus was willing to risk His reputation to save theirs. He was willing to go against the grain of religious leaders to liberate women from centuries of oppressive pious tradition. He delivered women from diseases and set them free from spiritual darkness. He took the fearful and forgotten and transformed them into the faithful and forever remembered. "Truly I tell you," Jesus said, "wherever this gospel is preached throughout the world, what she has done will also be told, in memory of her" (Matthew 26:13).

Jesus saw women as image bearers of God whom He came to save and then to send. He freed them from their painful pasts and freed them to fulfill His purposeful plans. He made no distinction between male or female, married or single, old or young. He simply related to people in regard to their relationship to God or lack of one.

Just as surely as Jesus overturned the money changers' tables in the temple, He overturned the exploitation and mistreatment of women (Matthew 21:12; Mark 11:15; John 2:15). Not only did He accept the women as they were, but also He challenged them to become more. Even though He didn't give explicit instructions on the specific roles of men and women, He taught by example. Jesus spoke with, mingled with, ministered to, and taught women just as easily as He did His male followers.

He didn't limit His teaching illustrations to male-only experiences, but He clarified His principles with examples from women's lives as well. He compared God's joy over a lost soul coming to faith to the joy of a woman finding a lost coin (Luke 15:8-10). He taught of persistence in prayer by comparing it to a determined woman knocking on her neighbor's door (Luke 18:1-8). He compared heaven to yeast that a woman mixes into a large amount of flour until it works all through the dough (Matthew 13:33).

While spending time getting to know the women who encountered Jesus in the New Testament, we've seen how Jesus shone the spotlight on particular women to point out exemplary living, gracious giving, bold believing, winsome worship, and fastidious faith. We saw Jesus pause in the middle of His busy day for the bleeding woman, stop His teaching to lift the chin of the bent and bowed, walk miles to deliver one little girl from demons, and wait patiently in the hot noon sun for the broken Samaritan to arrive. What kind of God does that? A God who loves His daughters.

He took the fearful and forgotten and
transformed them into the faithful
and forever remembered.

EMBRACING FREEDOM
TO BE AND TO DO

As I mentioned in the beginning, what Jesus did to lift up women has not been duplicated in any other world religion. Even today in Middle Eastern countries, women are often veiled in thick black chadors or burkas. Their faces are covered, their identities hidden. Some are not allowed to be educated. Others are not allowed to work outside the home. Watch news footage from these countries. Look at the streets during the busiest parts of the day. Women are conspicuously absent.

Many critics of Christianity suggest that women have been suppressed and oppressed in the church by encouraging male domination. And while that may be true in some cases, we cannot blame that on Jesus. He honored and respected women at every turn. He called them out of hiding and validated them as "daughters of Abraham."

Pastor Erwin Lutzer of Moody Bible Church, along with his wife, Rebecca, wrote: "Jesus affirmed and validated women as equal partners in the family of God, which He came to establish. He proclaimed liberty to the captive. He did so, in part, by countering the debilitating cultural bias against women. Jesus clearly created a new family of brothers and sisters who shared the same heavenly Father (Mark 3:21-35). Thus, as members of the new family, women must have equality of spiritual privilege."[1]

I am captivated by words of freedom Jesus spoke to the women we have visited. "Woman, you are set free from your infirmity," Jesus told the crippled woman (Luke 13:12). "Daughter, your faith has healed you. Go in peace and be freed from your suffering," Jesus assured the woman with the chronic flow of blood (Mark 5:34). "Then neither do I condemn you...Go now and leave your life of sin," He said to the woman caught in adultery (John 8:11). All through the New Testament we see Jesus flinging prison doors open wide and brave women walking into freedom. Oh, that we would do the same. "It is for freedom that Christ has set us free" (Galatians 5:1).

How proud I am of those women who accepted Jesus' invitation to come out of hiding. They were change agents who listened to the call of God above the oppressive voices of the culture. When it comes right down to it, it was the women who got it. The woman with the alabaster box understood that no matter what anyone thinks of us, Jesus deserves our worship. The woman at the well understood that no matter how broken our lives may be, Jesus is the long-awaited Messiah who makes all things new. Mary of Bethany understood that regardless of other people's expectations on our lives, spending time with Jesus is the most valuable choice we can make. Martha understood that regardless of the tragedy of present circumstances, Jesus is the Son of God who has power over life and death. These women understood Jesus' true identity when those closest to Him did not. The women were the ones who offered spiritual stamina with their presence and walked with Jesus until the very end, even at personal risk to themselves.

He emerged from the baptismal waters to wash away the boundary lines that kept women out of religious life in general. From Mary of Nazareth to Mary of Magdala, God used women to accomplish His divine purposes. Brave women stepped forward. Courageous women spoke up. Committed women joined hands.

Jesus is proof that God loves us. "A woman's high-calling as God's image bearer renders her incapable of insignificance, no matter what has gone wrong in her life or how much she has lost."[2] In our time together, we have met several women whose lives were impacted by Jesus. We've met a mother, two sisters, and a little girl. We've met single women, married women, and divorced women. We've met women who made mistakes and women who were mistreated. We've met women who had been beaten down by life and pushed aside by prejudice.

While these women may have lived many years ago, they are really no different from you and me. Each one had hopes and dreams, fears and concerns, victories and defeats. And in each case, their dreams were laid shattered in a thousand tiny pieces before them…until Jesus. And how did the women respond to Jesus calling them center stage?

- Mary of Nazareth *stepped up* to accept her calling.

- The woman with the chronic bleeding *spoke up* to tell of her miraculous healing.

- The woman caught in adultery *cleaned up* to start anew.

- The empty woman at the well *filled up* to evangelize an entire town.

- The woman with the alabaster jar *opened up* her heart to worship.

- Mary of Bethany *showed up* in the classroom.

- Martha *moved up* to the head of the class.

- The woman with the crippled back *walked up* to receive her healing.

- The Syrophoenician mother was *shored up* for bold believing.

- The widow *gave all up* as an example of sacrificial giving.

- Mary Magdalene *signed up* to join Jesus' ministry team.

These leading ladies' stories show us that in God's family, girls are important too. They were strong women of faith who were bolstered by Jesus to come out of the shadows and take their place among the world changers of their day.

I hope you have seen a bit of yourself in each of these women. I pray that you have written your name into the script. For, you see, their story is your story, their suffering is your suffering, their hope is your hope, their victory is your victory…it is Jesus. He's the focus of each of their stories and ours—the Hero who takes our breath away with His amazing love.

NOW IT'S YOUR TURN

God always has important kingdom work for us to do. We were not meant to be mere stagehands or decorative props, but leading ladies working together alongside our brothers to impact the world for Christ.

Every little girl needs to grow up knowing she is valued, that she is made in the image of God. Every little girl needs to grow up expectantly waiting for her God-given potential to be released. These women gave us a taste—a glimpse.

After Jesus' ascension, both men and women waited in Jerusalem for the promised Holy Spirit. On the day of Pentecost, as the Holy Spirit descended with a gusty wind and tongues of fire, Peter stood and explained to curious onlookers what was taking place.

> This is what was spoken by the prophet Joel: "In the last days, God says, I will pour out my Sprit on all people. Your sons and daughters will prophesy, your young men will see

visions, your old men will dream dreams. Even on my servants, both men and women, I will pour out my Spirit in those days, and they will prophesy" (Acts 2:16-18).

Peter explained to the people what Jesus had been showing them all along. God's grace, love, and power are extended to all people regardless of rank or race, gender or generation: sons and daughters, young and old, men and women. Paul would later pen: "There is neither Jew nor Gentile, neither slave nor free, nor is there male and female, for you are all one in Christ Jesus" (Galatians 3:28).

Where do we go from here? That is a question for you and God to decide. However, if God calls you center stage to accomplish His purpose for this generation, I pray you will accept the role of a lifetime. And who knows? Perhaps you are holding this book in your hand and being challenged to fulfill God's purposes "for such a time as this."

Every little girl needs to grow up knowing she is valued, that she is made in the image of God.

Bible Study Guide

Contents

A New Day for Women

In the pages of *Never Less Than*, we take a journey to look at the life of Jesus and His radical countercultural response to women during His 33 years of earthly ministry. We sit by the well with the Samaritan woman, expecting insult and rejection but receiving acceptance and love. We stand with the woman caught in adultery, expecting condemnation and death but finding forgiveness and a chance to start anew. We reach out our hand with the bleeding woman to touch the hem of Jesus' garment in secret, only to be healed and publicly affirmed. We rise from the ruins of life with Mary Magdalene and run with purpose to announce the miracle of Jesus' resurrection. But there is so much more to learn. My hope and prayer are that the words in this book will merely whet your appetite to learn more about the deep, deep love God has for His female image bearers.

Jesus came to set the captive free. That freedom was extended to women shackled by a patriarchal culture that cast them aside. He affirmed, validated, and honored women in God's family. Jesus broke cultural rules and spoke with, ministered to, and taught women just as readily as He did His male followers. He pulled women from the shadows and set them center stage to play leading roles in God's redemptive plan.

The numbered lessons in this Bible study guide coincide with the numbered chapters and expand upon one or more of the aspects covered. This study guide is for those who want to go deeper, learn more, and solidify their understanding of God's view of women. Let's get started.

Created for Divine Purpose

Because we began our journey in the book of Genesis, let's begin our Bible study there as well. Here is a wonderful quote I'd like you to ponder: "In majestic strokes and with cosmic vistas, the first page of the Bible sets forth the story of God's dealings with humankind within the designs of creation. The beginnings of human history are correlated to the beginnings of time itself, and human life is described as the glorious culmination of God's creative endeavors."[1] Now, open your Bible to Genesis 1.

1. Look closely at Genesis 1:26. What does it say about *who* created man?

   Who do you think is included in the "us"?

Read John 1:1-4 and note where Jesus was at creation.

2. What does Genesis 1 say about *how* God created man? How was this different from the manner in which He created everything prior? (Genesis 1:27; 2:7,21-22)

3. How was the nature of man different from all the other creatures God created? (Genesis 1:26)

Genesis 1:27 specifies that God created mankind, both male and female.

4. How was this reiterated in Genesis 5:1-2?

5. Man had a need and God met it by creating "a helper." The Hebrew word is *ezer* and means "one who comes along to rescue." What did Eve rescue Adam from?

6. After God created Eve, at the close of the sixth day, what did He say about all that He had made? (Genesis 1:31)

7. What was Adam and Eve's role in the garden? (Genesis 1:26,28)

8. Were any job descriptions or gender-specific delegations of duties given to Adam and Eve?

9. The disobedience of Adam and Eve, often referred to as the "fall," was certainly the most tragic event in history. Read Genesis 3:13-19 and list the results of the fall for the following: Man, Woman, and the Serpent.

10. Who did God say would eventually crush Satan's head? (Genesis 3:15)

The word "offspring" used here is the Hebrew word *zera*, which means "seed." If you remember from chapter 1, the ancient Greeks believed that a man's semen contained tiny humans and a woman's only role in procreation was to be the soil into which the seed was planted. However, in Genesis 3:15, God states that the offspring or seed of the woman would destroy the enemy. Scientists didn't discover that a woman had anything other than a passive role in procreation until 1827, when Carl Ernest von Baer discovered the human ovum and subsequently a woman's eggs. Isn't it exciting when science discovers what God has already told us?

Another thought on this verse: Genesis 3:15 (NKJV) was not clear on who "her Seed" was, but the rest of the Bible answers that question. We know how the story ends.

11. Who is the "Seed" that eventually crushed the enemy's head?

12. Now tell me, does woman have a significant role in God's plan of redemption?

13. Some have said that woman was the cause for the fall of mankind. However, what do the following New Testament verses tell us?

Romans 5:12-19

1 Corinthians 15:21-22

14. How did Adam and Eve's disobedience affect all mankind? (Romans 5:18-19)

15. What did Jesus come to do? (Matthew 20:28; John 10:10; Romans 5:18-19; 1 John 3:8)

16. Sin, death, fear, shame, guilt, doubt, and spiritual death entered the world through Adam and Eve. No longer did men and women live free and unashamed. They were now living in a darkened world, held captive by the consequences of sin. But Jesus came to set us free and restore what we had lost. What will ultimately set us free? (John 8:32)

    Truth is not simply a way of thinking or speaking. Truth is a person. What did Jesus say about His identity? (John 14:6)

    Combining these two verses, what works together to set us free?

17. Read and record Galatians 5:1. What does that mean to you?

Let's end today's lesson by praising God with the words of Psalm 118:6. Look up the verse and make it your prayer of praise today.

Blessed Through Radical Obedience

If there is one lesson we can learn from Mary, the mother of Jesus, it's the amazing impact of a person's obedience to God's call on her life. In this lesson, we will focus on the results of radical obedience.

1. Review Luke 1:26-45 and record Mary's response to Gabriel's message. Can you say that about yourself today?

2. What did Mary call herself in Luke 1:38?

The Greek word for "servant" that Mary used here is *doulos* or *doule* (the feminine form). It can also be translated "bondslave" or "bondservant," and is defined as "one who gives himself up to the will of another, without any idea of bondage."[2] It's becoming a servant by choice.

3. Read and record Elizabeth's summation of Mary's attitude toward God (Luke 1:45). Can you say that about yourself today?

4. Even though Gabriel described what was going to happen to Mary, I'm sure she didn't completely understand how this miracle would take place. Are there circumstances in your own life where you know God is working but you don't understand how the miracle could possibly take place? Explain.

5. Mary didn't understand completely, but she obeyed God totally. Why?

Read her song of praise recorded in Luke 1:46-55 and note what she knew about God's character and His ways.

6. It's difficult, if not impossible, to put that amount of trust in a

stranger. How does our level of knowledge of God relate to our level of trust in Him?

7. Mary tells us how to practice radical obedience in John 2. What did she say to the servants after she realized the wine was about to run out? (John 2:5)

8. Read Luke 5:1-10. What did Jesus tell Peter to do?

What was Peter's initial response?

Why did Peter obey?

What was the result of Peter's obedience?

Can you say what Peter said (verse 5)? If so, fill in this blank: "Lord, I don't understand why You are telling me to do this, but

_____,

I will do it."

9. If Mary were sitting beside you, I think she would say the same thing to you she said to the wine stewards in John 2:5. I know we've already recorded her words, but let's do it again. If you are willing to live a life of radical obedience to God, fill in the following blank with your name. Whatever God says, I, _____, will do.

If you wrote your name in that blank, hang on to your hat! God is about to take you to some amazing places!

LESSON 3

Loved as God's Daughter

In the Old Testament, God has many names. He is Elohim, the Creator; El Elyon, God Most High; El Roi, the God Who Sees; El Shaddai, the All-Sufficient One; Adonai, the Lord; Jehovah, the Self-Existent One; Jehovah-Jireh, the Lord Will Provide; Jehovah-Rapha, the Lord Who Heals; Jehovah-Shalom, the Lord Is Peace; Jehovah-Raah, the Lord My Shepherd...and many more.

But in the New Testament, we are invited to call God by a new name. It's the name Jesus referred to more than any other: Father. Let's turn our attention to our heavenly Father who loves His girls.

1. What did Jesus call the woman who had been bleeding for 12 years? (Matthew 9:22)

How do you think that word made her feel?

How does it make you feel knowing that God looks at you as His daughter?

2. Look up the following verses and note the references to God as our Father or you as His child.

2 Corinthians 6:18

Galatians 4:6-7 (Don't let it throw you that this verse talks about "sons." We're going to get to that in a moment.)

1 John 3:1

3. Read Ephesians 1:4-6 and note how we were brought into the family of God.

John MacArthur notes: "In ancient Rome, fathers chose a child for adoption when they were not able to have children of their own.

They adopted a son in order to have someone to carry on the family name and inherit their property. It was a legal relationship: All ties to the child's natural family were severed, and the child was placed in a new family with the same prestige and privileges of a natural child, including becoming an heir. If the child had any debt, it was immediately canceled. The adoption was a sealed process with many witnesses making it official."[3]

In modern times, most adoptions are of babies. However, in biblical, times adoption usually took place after the child was older and had proved to be fit to carry on the family name in a worthy manner.

4. Going back to Ephesians 1:4-6, when did God decide to adopt you?

What did you do to deserve being adopted as God's daughter? (Ephesians 2:8-9)

At what point was your adoption made final or legally binding? (Ephesians 1:13-14)

5. Go back up to the explanation of adoption: "If the child had any debt, it was immediately canceled." How was your debt canceled? (1 Peter 3:18)

Now let's talk about the word *sons.* The Hebrew word *son* does not necessarily mean "male offspring." In the Old Testament, the word *ben* can mean a son or a daughter. Remember from lesson 1, Genesis 1 says that God created man, meaning humans. Then the Word says, "Male and female he created them" (Genesis 1:27). The word *son* can mean the offspring of a human. It does not always mean a male child.

In the New Testament Greek, the word *huios* is translated "son." And like the Hebrew word *ben,* it can mean a male child or it can refer to offspring, both male and female.

The apostle Paul wrote to the Galatians, "You are all children of God through faith, for all of you who were baptized into Christ have clothed yourselves with Christ. There is neither Jew nor Gentile, neither slave nor free, nor is there male and female, for you are all one in Christ Jesus" (Galatians 3:26-28).

6. What does that teach us about Paul's use of the word "sons"?

Here's another wonderful aspect of being called a "son of God." In those days, only male offspring could inherit the father's wealth, but not so in God's family.

7. What does Paul call us women in Romans 8:16-17?

And here's more good news for you, God's daughter. You never have to worry about the stock market going down or the economy crashing to ruin your inheritance. Our Abba Father has already given us a taste of our inheritance that is to come.

8. What does the book of 1 Peter tell us about the safety of our inheritance as a child of God? (1 Peter 1:3-4)

9. What do you learn about this "down payment" or "deposit" in Ephesians 1:13-14?

10. What are you doing with that part of your inheritance? Are you investing wisely?

11. You are constantly on your heavenly Father's mind. How does Isaiah 49:15-16 assure you of that truth?

12. Read and record David's prayer in Psalm 17:8.

The term "apple of your eye" refers to the pupil of the eye. The pupil is necessary for sight and must be protected. That is how God sees you! You are the apple of His eye, and He will protect you.

David also refers to God's protection: "Hide me in the shadow of your wings." This was a common Hebrew metaphor for protection against oppression, as shade protects from the oppressive heat of the hot desert sun.

13. What picture comes to mind when you think of hiding under the shadow of your heavenly Father's wings?

14. What can separate you from the love of your heavenly Father? (Romans 8:38-39)

15. Read and record Isaiah 54:10. What will never be shaken?

I love the words "unfailing love." The Hebrew word is *hesed* and often translated "loving-kindness," "steadfast love," "grace," "mercy," "faithfulness," "goodness," and "devotion." *Hesed* is used 240 times in the Old Treatment and is considered one of the most important words in the vocabulary of the Old Testament. Why? Because God's unfailing love is one of the most important themes of the entire Bible. It's who He is and what He does.

Isaiah 54:10 also states that God has "compassion" on you. The Hebrew word for "compassion" is *racham*, which means, as Beth

Moore notes, "to soothe; to cherish; to love deeply like parents; to be compassionate, to be tender…the verb usually refers to a strong love which is rooted in some kind of natural bond, often from a superior one to an inferior one. [Here's the best part.] Small babies evoke this feeling."[4]

If you're a mother, what feelings came over you when you looked at your babies? (To be on the safe side, think of them when they were sleeping.)

That is the word *racham*. That is how God feels about you! And the good news is, God continues to feel that way about us even when we grow up.

16. Describe how that makes you feel.

17. Like all good fathers, our heavenly Father has dreams for His daughters. What does Jeremiah 29:11-12 tell you about God's plan for your life?

In conclusion, let's end today's lesson by basking in the light of God's great love for His daughters. Look up the following verses and note what you learn about God's love for you. Put a check mark beside the one that means the most to you and share why that is.

Psalm 13:5-6

Psalm 36:5

Psalm 63:3-4

John 3:16

John 15:13

Romans 5:5,8

Ephesians 5:1

1 John 3:1

1 John 4:10

Valued in Jesus' Teaching

During Jesus' day, women blended in with the background of society, but He pulled them center stage in the drama of redemption and gave them leading roles in the most important scenes of history. Earlier in the book, we sat roadside as Jesus interacted with several women in the New Testament. We saw how He highly valued women in a culture that valued women very little. Today, let's focus on how Jesus treated a woman caught in adultery who was used by the Pharisees as bait to try to trick Jesus.

1. As a review, read John 8:1-11. Would you say that Jesus spoke to the woman caught in adultery with compassion or contempt?

How was Jesus' treatment toward this woman vastly different from that of the Pharisees?

2. One way Jesus showed He valued women was in His teachings on sexual sin and marriage. As we see in the story of the woman caught in adultery, there was a double standard when it came to sexual sin. Women were considered seductive and usually blamed for men's lusts and adulterous relationships. Read Matthew 5:27-29 and note what Jesus said about sexual sin. Also note where He placed the blame.

How did this teaching go against the cultural norms?

How was Jesus protecting women and removing the double standard?

On whom was Jesus placing responsibility for lust?

3. The way women were devalued is also demonstrated by the ease with which a man could divorce his wife. As Erwin and Rebecca Lutzer note, "A man only had to clap his hands three times to

legally divorce his wife for something as trivial as burning the bread."[5] However, Jesus spoke against this practice that devalued women.

Read Matthew 19:1-9 and note what Jesus said about divorce.

While this sounds logical to us in the twenty-first century, what was the disciples' response to Jesus' statement about divorce? (Matthew 19:10)

How did Jesus' teaching on divorce protect and value women?

4. What do you see added to Jesus' response to the Pharisees' question in Mark 10:2? (See Mark 10:3-9)

In those days, only a man could divorce his wife, not vice versa. How did Jesus' response go against the grain of the culture?

5. Later, Paul would write some revolutionary ideas for marriage. Read 1 Corinthians 7:1-5. How do these verses contrast with the

commonly accepted belief of the day, when women were the property of their husbands?

Paul uses the words "in the same way" in 1 Corinthians 7:4. What would that have meant to a wife of those days who had previously had literally no rights in her marriage?

6. As mentioned in chapter 1, women in ancient Greece were considered a husband's property and were treated as such. Read Ephesians 5:25-33 and note Paul's teaching on how a husband should love and treat his wife. How did Christ show love toward the church?

How was this radically different from the culture of Jesus' day, which viewed women as a commodity?

This would be a good time to look at how Jesus valued women in every aspect of His teaching. Luke mentioned women in his Gospel more often than Matthew, Mark, or John. He showed how Jesus treated women with worth and dignity by referring to them in His parables and highlighting their actions as godly examples to emulate.

Jesus not only crossed gender boundaries to teach women, but He also clarified His teaching with incidents from women's lives as

He taught others. Look at the following parables and note if Jesus used a male or female as the main character. I'll get you started.

Luke 13:18-19 A *man* who planted a mustard seed.

Luke 13:20-21 A *woman* who

Luke 15:1-7

Luke 15:8-10

Luke 18:1-8

Luke 18:10-14

7. In a culture that devalued and ignored women, what was Jesus teaching by example as He referred to both women and men in His teachings?

8. Luke also showed an alternating pattern of Jesus healing men and women with similar ailments. Look up the following and notice the male/female healings and the similarities of their conditions.

Luke 6:6-11 and 13:10-13

Luke 7:11-16 and 8:40-42,51-55

Luke 8:1-2 and 8:26-33

Luke 5:12-16 and 8:40-47

What does this show you about Jesus' countercultural attitude toward the value of women?

Even before Jesus began His teachings and miracles, we see another pairing of a man and a woman. Even at the very beginning of Jesus' life, we see that God is doing something new.

9. Who prophesied over the baby Jesus in the temple? (Luke 2:25-38)

Read Luke 12:6-7. In a culture that placed little value on women, how do you think these words made the female listeners feel?

10. Now, let's go back to our sister standing before Jesus, expecting condemnation but receiving grace and forgiveness. Read the following verses and note what you learn about God's forgiveness.

Ephesians 2:8-9

Ephesians 4:32

Colossians 2:13-14

Colossians 3:13

This is one way that a *relationship* with Jesus differs from a *religion.* "Religion says you do what is right in order to earn acceptance, love and forgiveness. A relationship with God through Jesus Christ is not based on our performance because we already are accepted, loved and forgiven."[6]

11. Read the following verses and note what happens once you ask God to forgive you.

Hebrews 10:17

2 Corinthians 5:17

1 John 1:9

12. Did the woman caught in adultery have to do anything to earn her forgiveness?

13. What is God's final verdict for the repentant Christian? (Romans 8:1)

Receiving grace and forgiveness for the wrongs we have committed is an act of faith. "It is difficult to fathom such extravagant unconditional love, yet so many of us leave His gift unopened. We admire its wrapping or marvel at its enormity but avoid getting too close. Something within us cannot grasp the idea that God meant this for us, so we put conditions on accepting His gift."[7]

We all have regrets—just different ones. The Bible says, "All have sinned and fall short of the glory of God" (Romans 3:23). God is offering you the same forgiveness He offered the woman caught in adultery. Have you accepted that forgiveness?

Restored Through Jesus' Ministry

Every woman we meet in the Gospels was changed by Jesus. Some were healed, some were forgiven, some were delivered, and some were freed. But not one woman remained the same as she was before her life intersected with His. Jesus changed empty to full, rejected to accepted, and broken to whole. Let's take a seat by the well and listen in on His conversation with the Samaritan woman He came to save.

EMPTY TO FULL

1. Read John 4:1-42. The Samaritan woman we meet here was as empty as the water pot she carried on her head. What about her conversation with Jesus hints at the emptiness she felt in her heart?

Look up the definition of *empty* in the dictionary and note its meaning.

2. Has there ever been a time in your life when you felt empty? How did you try to fill that emptiness? What was the result of your efforts?

3. Jesus offered to fill the empty woman at the well with living water. He offers that same living water to anyone who will receive it. Read Revelation 22:17. What are the Spirit and the bride urging all to do?

4. Blaise Pascal once said, "There is a God-shaped vacuum in the heart of every man which cannot be filled by any created thing, but only by God, the Creator, made known through Jesus." How has this proved true in your own life?

REJECTED TO ACCEPTED

5. Feelings of rejection often come from empty, lonely lives. Because of death, divorce, and deferred marriage, an estimated 36 million Americans live alone.[8] Many of the women we meet in *Never Less Than* struggled with feelings of rejection. What does the Bible teach about God's unconditional acceptance?

Romans 5:8

1 John 4:10

1 John 4:19

Let's consider the following quote by Mark Rutland in his book, *Streams of Mercy.*

> Jesus stands behind the communion table with His nail-scarred hands outstretched and the light of mercy in His eyes. His voice, His words meet us with healing warmth as we drag our waterlogged burdens up the rocky shoreline from life's most chilling seas. "I love you," He whispers. "I forgive you. Come and dine."[9]

Not only have we been totally and completely accepted by God; we have also been pursued by Him. In our eyes we may see ourselves as pleading with God to accept us. The truth is, Jesus is standing at the door pursuing us. He longs to come in.

6. Read and record Revelation 3:20.

7. As a review, read and record John 4:4. Why is this verse significant?

8. God was pursuing this woman, and He sent His Son on special assignment. He does the same for you! How does the idea that God pursues a relationship with you make you feel about your value and worth?

9. See Genesis 3:9. What was the first question asked in the Bible? What does that show you about God's desire to have a relationship with His children?

BROKEN TO WHOLE

The Samaritan woman we meet at the well was no doubt broken by her circumstances and her inability to make life work on her own. Many of the women we read about in the Gospels were broken people—broken women whom Jesus made whole. I think one of the ways we can better picture what brokenness looks like is to think of ourselves as vessels created by God.

10. Read Jeremiah 18:3-4. What do you learn about the Potter and the clay?

11. Read the following verses and note what you learn about the relationship between the Potter and the clay.

Deuteronomy 32:6

Psalm 119:73

Psalm 139:13

Isaiah 44:2

Isaiah 64:8

Now that we know God formed us, let's consider what happens when our particular pottery gets chipped, cracked, or broken.

12. Look up the definition of *broken* and note its meaning.

13. How did David feel about his life at the time he wrote Psalm 31:12?

What do you think he meant by that?

14. Let's consider the following quote by Meister Eckhart in *The Spirituality of the Imperfection*, written almost 700 years ago: "Imperfection is the crack in the armor, the 'wound' that lets God in." Paraphrase that in your own words.

Do you feel broken in any area of your life: physically, spiritually, or emotionally?

15. Read Isaiah 61:1-3. What did Jesus come to do? (Jesus read part of this in the synagogue at Nazareth, recorded in Luke 4:18-19.)

16. Samuel Chadwick said, "It is a wonder what God can do with a broken heart, if He gets all the pieces." How did Jesus take the broken pieces of the following women's lives and make them whole?

Mary Magdalene

The woman with the 12-year hemorrhage

The woman caught in adultery

The Samaritan woman at the well

As we have looked at what it means to be broken, let me tell you what brokenness is not. Brokenness is not about being sad and gloomy all the time. Brokenness is not about feeling sorry for yourself. Brokenness is not about being wounded by someone's actions or words and refusing to heal. Brokenness is not about experiencing a tragedy and allowing the pain to define your life.

Now, all of those things can lead to brokenness, but they do not define it. Brokenness is a matter of the heart. It's a giving up of our control and handing the reins to God. It's saying, "I can't do this on my own," and then trusting Him to take complete control. That's why the poor in spirit can be happy.

Jesus came to bind up the brokenhearted. But that's not all. He takes the broken pieces of our lives and makes a beautiful mosaic—something more beautiful than we could ever have imagined. Jesus fills our empty spaces and moves into our hollow places.

Welcomed into God's Presence

As we discovered earlier in the book, the Jewish synagogues and temples were set up to separate men and women, Jew and Gentile, common folk and holy men according to the prejudices of the day. How did God feel about those man-made separations? Let's find out. Join me now as we walk into a roomful of men with a sinful woman who came to worship Jesus.

1. Read Luke 7:36-50. How is the woman with the alabaster jar described?

Would she have been welcomed in such a gathering? Why or why not?

What was Jesus' reaction to her display of worship?

What was her attitude? Was she humble or prideful?

What was Simon's attitude? Was he humble or prideful?

Which person reflects your attitude the most?

Did Jesus welcome her worship or turn her away?

2. Read the parable of the tax collector and the Pharisee in Luke 18:9-14. What similarities do you see between these scenarios?

In our last lesson, we looked at what it means to be broken. No doubt the sinful woman who anointed Jesus with perfume fit that description. Generally, broken people are more concerned with what God thinks than with what people think. They tend to be open and transparent because they have nothing to lose.

3. How did the woman who anointed Jesus' feet show that she cared more about what God thought than what people thought?

4. Would you say that you care more about what God thinks of you than what other people think of you?

5. What are some reasons you think men and women are reluctant to show outward displays of worship?

6. One stumbling block to showing outward displays of worship is pride. How did Simon's thoughts reveal his prideful attitude?

7. Read the following verses and note what God really thinks about pride.

   Proverbs 3:34

Proverbs 16:5

Proverbs 18:12

Luke 1:50-52

James 4:6

8. How does Jesus' encounter with the woman who anointed Him paint a beautiful picture of James 4:10?

9. What does the Bible tell us about praising God for who He is and thanking Him for what He does?

1 Chronicles 16:8-10

1 Chronicles 16:34

Psalm 30:11-12

Psalm 100:4-5

Psalm 107:1,8

10. Read Romans 1:21. What did the writer of the letter to the Romans note as one of the reasons for God's wrath? What did the people fail to do?

11. Much of Herod's Temple was different from the original tabernacle, but it still had the Holy of Holies. Read Matthew 27:51-53 and answer the following questions.

Describe what happened in the temple when Jesus died.

How was the curtain (veil) torn?

Who do you think tore it?

Read Hebrews 10:19-22. What is the significance of the veil separating sinful mankind from God being torn?

In the temple, there was a partition separating the Jews from the Gentiles, and another one that separated the Jewish women from the Jewish men.

12. What did Paul say Jesus did to that physical wall that represented a spiritual separation of Jew and Gentile? (Ephesians 2:13-18)

13. Now who can enter God's presence and with what attitude? (Hebrews 4:15-16; 10:19-22)

Why can we enter God's presence with confidence?

Just as Jesus welcomed the woman with the alabaster jar into His presence, God welcomes us into His. Close out today's lesson by writing a note of thanks to God for loving you enough to make that possible.

Invited into Jesus' Classroom

During the time of Jesus, most rabbis thought it was inappropriate to teach women. While men were expected to attend synagogue and study the Torah, women were not. A common belief was that men learn, but women merely listen. Women were treated as unteachable creatures. However, Jesus taught where women could hear, and He even commended women who crossed cultural and gender boundaries to learn Scripture. Let's spend this lesson exploring why it's so important for a woman to know God and His Word.

1. Read Genesis 3:1-3. What was Eve's core problem? Did she know the truth?

2. What can happen when we do not know God's truth? (Ephesians 4:14-15)

3. What did Moses pray in Exodus 33:13?

The Hebrew word for *know*, which is used here, is a relational word. It's the same word that is translated "know" in the King James Version that says, "Adam knew Eve his wife; and she conceived" (Genesis 4:1). It's more than head knowledge. It's a knowing that leads to a relationship between God and the learner. It is "the meeting and marriage between ourselves and God…the highest and holiest happiest hope of the human heart, the thing we were all born hungering for, hunting for, longing for."[10]

This is too good to pass up. Read Exodus 33:17.

4. What was God's reply to Moses' request?

Friend, that is His reply to your hunger to know Him as well.

5. In the Old Testament, women were expected to be present at the reading of the Torah (Scriptures). Read the following and note Moses' command.

Deuteronomy 31:9-13

Nehemiah 8:1-3

Somewhere in the 400 years that spanned the Old Testament and the New Testament, women were shunned from the classroom. The layout of Herod's Temple reinforced what the religious leaders believed: Some people were more worthy of closer access to God than others.

It's difficult, if not impossible, to trust someone you don't know. It's difficult to have faith in someone who is only an acquaintance. Faith requires a steady diet of the truth to remain strong.

6. What did David say is one benefit of knowing God? (Psalm 9:10)

7. What did the psalmist long for in the following verses? (Psalm 119:12,18,97,103,105)

8. What do we discover the psalmist knew about God in the following verses? (Psalm 20:6; 25:10; 100:3; 119:68,75-76)

Part of knowing God involves understanding His character and His ways. How would you like to see a job description for God? While our finite minds cannot comprehend His infinite role, He gives us a tiny glimpse in the book of Job as He replies to Job's many questions regarding the tragedy of his life. Read Job 38–41 and note what you learn about God. You may want to spread this assignment out over a few days and savor God's description of Himself.

RAHAB

Let's take a look at one woman whose knowledge of God radically affected her future and future generations in her family tree. Read Joshua 2 and answer the following question.

The Israelites were finally ready to enter the Promised Land. Where did the spies go once they entered Jericho?

The idea of the spies going to a prostitute's house might be a little disconcerting. Here's what the *NIV Commentary* has to say: "The house of the prostitute Rahab was the only place where the men could stay with any hope of remaining undetected and where they would be able to gather the information they were seeking. Moreover, her house afforded an easy way of escape since it was located on the wall."[11] In those days, it wasn't uncommon for traveling men to stay in the house of a prostitute. The people of Jericho would not be suspicious of the men staying there. (I'm just glad we have hotels these days.)

9. What did Rahab say to the spies about God? (verses 8-13)

10. How did her knowledge of God spare her life and the life of her family? (Joshua 2:14; 6:22-23)

11. Because of Rahab's faith in and knowledge of God, she was grafted into the Hebrew nation. Who were some of her more famous descendants? (Matthew 1:5-16)

Rahab had been a prostitute in a heathen nation, but because of her knowledge of God and her faith in Him, He showcased her as one of His mighty warriors in the Hall of Faith. Peruse the Hall of Faith in Hebrews 11 and find her name engraved on its walls.

12. Rahab had a good understanding of who God is. If someone were to ask you the question "Who is God?" what would you say?

13. How does knowing God affect your life? What difference has it made?

14. When we become students of God's Word, we are not left alone to try to understand the Scriptures the best we can. Who comes alongside us to help us understand what God is teaching us through His Word? (John 16:13)

15. We can read a menu and even look at and smell a buffet, but until we actually put the food in our mouths and digest it, we will still go hungry. We won't know if the food is good until we taste it. What did David challenge us to do? Read and record Psalm 34:8. Then rewrite that verse in your own words.

16. Jesus came to set women free, but with that freedom comes great responsibility. We must study the Word of God and learn how to handle it accurately. What did Paul encourage Timothy to do? (2 Timothy 2:15)

17. Earlier in the book, we took an in-depth look at how God welcomed Mary of Bethany into the classroom, recorded in Luke 10:38-42. As a review, how was she willing to go against the cultural norms of an all-male classroom?

18. What did Jesus say about Mary's choice to sit at the Teacher's feet to learn?

19. What did John write was his greatest joy? (3 John 4)

20. Sum up what it means to you that Jesus swung open the doors and invited women to join the classroom.

Affirmed in God's Family

In our previous lesson, we focused on how Jesus welcomed women into His classroom. We left Martha in the kitchen, but is that where she stayed? What does God consider a woman's most important role? Where does a woman find her significance? We'll answer all those questions and more, but let's start out with seeing how knowing Jesus changed Martha's life.

In order to review what we learned about Martha, read Luke 10:38-42 again. Looking at various Bible translations, Martha is described as bothered, worried, encumbered, captive, and busy—basically a jittery type.

1. What caused her to feel so burdened?

2. Did you notice that Martha tried to place her burden on Mary's

shoulders? Have you ever felt worried and bothered about a situation and then tried to alleviate your burden by placing it on someone else? (I know that is an uncomfortable question, but please be honest.) What does that look like in your life?

3. Perhaps you have felt the weight of someone else's yoke placed on *you*. What does that feel like? (Let me tell you a little secret: False guilt sometimes holds that yoke in place.)

Martha had a yoke around her neck and tried to get Mary to slip into the position of the second ox.

4. What is a yoke? Look it up in the dictionary and draw a picture of a yoke fit for two oxen.

5. What happens when we yoke ourselves to Jesus rather than to others' expectations of what we should be doing? (Matthew 11:28-30)

The New International Version states that Martha was "distracted" (Luke 10:40). The word can also mean "pulled apart" or "pulled away." Martha no doubt felt cultural pressure to perform in a certain way. Let's ask ourselves some personal questions to help evaluate our priorities.

6. Who created Martha's to-do list?

7. Who determines your to-do list?

8. Who determined Jesus' to-do list? (Mark 1:35-38; John 14:31)

9. How much of what Martha was doing was necessary?

10. How much of what you do is necessary?

11. What pulls you away from making time with Jesus your highest priority?

As women, we can make ourselves very busy doing good things. However, when we let God establish our priorities, we are set free to do great things.

12. How did Paul say we could determine what is "best" for our lives? (Philippians 1:9-11)

13. What can we learn about what happened to Martha after her encounter with Jesus? Did she accept His invitation and join the classroom? Look at her conversation with Jesus after her brother, Lazarust. Read John 11:20-27 and answer the following questions.

What did Jesus teach Martha?

This is one of the most fundamental truths of the Christian faith and is often repeated at funerals to give hope to those left behind…and it was given to a woman.

What did Jesus ask Martha?

How did Jesus asking Martha this question go against the culture norms and show that women must also learn?

What was her response?

How was her response similar to Peter's response recorded in Matthew 16:16?

In Jesus' response to Peter, He said, "Blessed are you, Simon son of Jonah, for this was not revealed to you by flesh and blood, but by my Father in heaven. And I tell you that you are Peter [Greek, *petros*, meaning "little rock or stone"], and on this rock [Greek, *petra*, meaning "big rock"] I will build my church, and the gates of Hades will not overcome it" (Matthew 16:17-18).

14. How exciting that one of the foundational truths of our faith was voiced by both a man and a woman. How precious that God made sure both statements were included in the Bible. Why is that significant against this particular cultural backdrop?

15. Did Martha become comfortable with Mary being Mary and letting Martha be Martha? (Hint: See John 12:2).

During Jesus' day, a woman's significance was wrapped up in being a wife and a mother. In many cases, that attitude is not much different today. But Jesus taught that a woman's significance wasn't dependent on either role. Her significance was wrapped up in who she was as a child of God (Luke 11:27-28).

Jesus didn't speak about being single specifically, but there were several significant people in His life who were never married. As far as we know, neither Mary nor Martha was married. Jesus Himself was single.

16. Paul spoke specifically to single women. What did he tell them? (1 Corinthians 7:32-35)

(Don't get hung up on Paul's idea that it is good to stay single. In 1 Timothy 4:1-3, he wrote that in the latter days "some will abandon the faith and follow deceiving spirits and things taught by demons. Such teachings come through hypocritical liars, whose consciences have been seared as with a hot iron. They forbid people to marry." Paul didn't teach not to marry; rather, he simply saw that an unmarried person would be better able to concentrate all his or her energies on building the kingdom. But I love marriage! So does God. It was His idea.)

17. Let's see what Jesus had to say about where a woman's significance came from. Read Luke 11:27-28.

What did the woman in the crowd cry out?

What was Jesus' response?

What can you surmise is a woman's most fulfilling role in life?

In Jesus' response, He catapulted women to the position of disciple, along with the men who had followed Him all along. He made it clear that a woman's significance rested in being a child of God.

18. When God created Adam and Eve, He commanded them, "Be fruitful and multiply, and fill the earth, and subdue it" (Genesis 1:28 NASB). In the New Testament, Jesus also talked about being fruitful and multiplying, but in a different sense. What did Jesus tell His disciples to do? (Matthew 28:18-20)

19. Jesus commissions all of us to share the gospel. Read the following verses and note what a Christ follower is often called.

2 Corinthians 6:18

Ephesians 5:1

1 John 3:1

How can each of us be fruitful and multiply in the kingdom of God?

20. Colossians 2:10 says the following: "In Him you have been made complete" (NASB). What does it mean to you to be complete in Christ?

21. Ponder these words by Carolyn Custis James: "A woman's high calling as God's image bearer renders her incapable of insignificance, no matter what has gone wrong in her life or how much she has lost."[12] What does that mean to you?

In no way is this lesson intended to diminish the importance of being a wife and a mother. Those have been two of the most important roles of my life. Being an *ezer* to my husband is an honor I do not take lightly. Being a mother to my son has been one of my greatest joys. To think that God gives a mother the privilege of shaping and molding a child, an eternal soul, for a very short, very fleeting time is simply mind-boggling. But if our significance is wrapped up in any person other than God and in who we are as His child, we will be disappointed and dissatisfied.

Write a summary statement about what determines your true significance as a woman.

Called Out of the Shadows

Earlier we took a bird's-eye view of women Jesus restored in His ministry. Today, let's zoom in on one particular woman to see how God called her out of the shadows and onto center stage. In chapter 9, we spend some time with the woman with the crippled back. Today, let's go back to the synagogue and take a closer look at the verbs or action words used in that passage. Read Luke 13:10-17 to refresh your memory. Concentrate on the actions of Jesus.

JESUS SAW HER

First of all, Jesus saw her even though she did not see Him. Read the following verses and note what you learn about what or whom God sees.

Psalm 33:13-15,18

Psalm 121:3-4,7-8

Matthew 6:3-4,6

1. Hagar was a young woman in a terrible situation. She was pregnant and mistreated by the only family she had. Read Genesis 16.

   What did Hagar call God after the angel had spoken to her?

   El Roi means "the God Who Sees." What does that particular name for God mean to you?

   How does the fact that God sees you make you feel?

   What did David say about what God sees? (Psalm 139)

2. No matter what you are going through today, know this: God sees you. He has not forgotten you. What reassurance does He give us in the words of Isaiah 49:15-16?

JESUS CALLED HER FORWARD

The Greek word for "called," *kaleo,* means "to call or invite." But it also means a spiritual calling to salvation, serving God and fellow believers. Read the following verses and note what you learn about your calling as a believer.

Romans 1:4-6

1 Corinthians 1:9

1 Thessalonians 2:11-12

1 Thessalonians 4:7

2 Timothy 1:8-10

1 Peter 2:9

2 Peter 1:3

3. Fulfilling a calling (or accepting God's invitation) usually involves getting out of our comfort zones. In my own life, I can't think of a time when obeying Him didn't. How did each one of the following women have to move out of their comfort zones to follow God?

Sarah, the wife of Abraham (Genesis 12:1)

Ruth (Ruth 2:1-3)

Esther (Esther 4, focusing on verses 12-16)

Mary Magdalene (Luke 8:1-3)

The woman with the 12-year bleeding (Luke 8:43-48)

Mary of Bethany (Luke 10:38-39)

The woman with the crippled back (Luke 13:12)

The Samaritan woman at the well (John 4:28-30)

I am sure the crippled woman felt very insignificant. I'm sure she felt like a nobody. And in the eyes of the world, that's exactly what she was. But to Jesus, she was a precious jewel.

4. Are you operating in your comfort zone, or have you ventured out to areas where you are totally dependent on God's power and might?

5. Why do you think God moves us out of our comfort zones to accomplish great feats for Him? Return to what Paul says about weakness versus strength as you read and record 2 Corinthians 12:9-10.

6. Read Hebrews 11:8 and note how Abraham responded to God's

call. Do you think this woman knew why Jesus was calling her forward? And yet what did she do?

7. What is the assurance for all of us who are called? (Romans 8:28)

JESUS TOUCHED HER

I love the thought of Jesus' hands reaching out and touching the people He came in contact with. The leprous outcast, the unclean recluse, the deceased son, the dead little girl…each person Jesus touched was changed by the hands of heaven, the fingertips of God. Look up the following verses and note the people Jesus touched and what happened to them.

Matthew 8:2-3,14-15

Matthew 9:27-30

Mark 7:31-35

Luke 7:11-15

Luke 8:51-55

Jesus healed people with His words. "Be clean!" He spoke to the man who suffered from leprosy (Matthew 8:3). He healed him physically with His words, but I believe Jesus healed the hurt in his soul with His touch. Can you think of a time when someone's touch ministered to you? A hug? A pat on the back? A touch of the hand?

Jesus touched the untouchables of the world. Will you do the same?

JESUS AFFIRMED HER

Jewish men were often called "sons of Abraham," but it was unheard of for a Jewish woman to be called a "daughter of Abraham." Once again, Jesus showed the world that women were just as valuable as men in the kingdom of God.

8. What did Jesus call the woman with the crippled back? (Luke 13:16)

9. How would it have affirmed her to know that Jesus stopped right in the middle of His teaching to take notice of her?

10. Read Romans 8:16 and note what God calls you.

JESUS HEALED HER

There is much we could say about Jesus healing people, but there is one specific aspect I want us to look at together. Read Matthew 14:14.

11. How did Jesus feel when He saw the crowds that had followed Him?

The Bible says, "He had compassion on them." The Greek word used for "compassion" in this passage is *splanchnizomai*. If you happen to be in the medical profession, that word might look familiar. Splanchnology is the study of the visceral parts—in common terms, the gut. The verb "carries the idea of being moved in the inner parts of the body. The ancients thought of the inward parts of the body as being the seat of emotions. In English, we usually refer to the 'heart,' but we also talk of a person having 'visceral' feelings; note how true compassion can affect us in the pit of our stomachs."[13]

12. Jesus felt the limp of the crippled woman. He felt the rejection of the woman at the well. He felt the loneliness of the woman labeled unclean because of bleeding. Does this give you a better idea of how His heart ached because of the sickness, heartache, and hunger He saw?

What does Hebrews 13:8 tell you about Him?

If Jesus felt *splanchnizomai,* gut-wrenching compassion, for the people He saw when He walked the earth, how does He feel about the pain you suffer today?

Dear friend, now I want you to picture yourself sitting behind the partition at the back of the temple with the woman with the crippled back. Jesus stops midsentence, sees *you,* calls to *you,* speaks to *you,* touches *your* soul to take away *your* pain, affirms *you* as a child of God, and then heals *you.* What feelings stir in your heart as you walk in her footsteps?

Highlighted in the Old Testament

I don't know about you, but like the Syrophoenician mother, I have fallen at Jesus' feet many times in prayer for the needs of my family. As a woman, it's what we do—bring our loved ones before God and pray for His intervention. As our Savior, it's what Jesus does—listens to our hearts and intercedes on our behalf. We have enjoyed getting to know many of the leading ladies of the New Testament. In this lesson, let's turn back time even further and meet a few of the leading ladies of the Old Testament.

RUTH

1. Read Ruth 1:1-5. From these five verses, list the six people you meet.

2. Now draw a line through those who had died by the end of verse 5. Who do you have left?

From the very beginning of the book of Ruth, we see that this is a story about women. While most of the other women in the Old Testament enter their particular stories on the arm of a man, we see these three women taking center stage alone. Continue reading verses 6-13.

3. What was Naomi's desire for her daughters-in-law?

4. Why did she want them to return to their homeland rather than continue on to Bethlehem with her?

5. What did the two daughters-in-law decide to do? (verses 14-18)

6. What does this tell you about the source of Ruth's identity and significance?

7. What did both Ruth and Naomi have in common?

8. Not only was Ruth a young widow; she was also apparently barren. What did this mean for her future?

9. Did she seem concerned? Why or why not?

10. How did Naomi view her present state? (verses 20-21)

Naomi felt as though God had forsaken her, but in reality He was working behind the scenes to put every detail in place. Why? Because God loves His daughters that much.

11. When Ruth went to glean in the fields the following day, where did she "just so happen" to go? (Ruth 2:1-9,19-20)

How did this revelation change Naomi's opinion about God? (verse 20)

12. Have you ever gone through a difficult time and felt God had deserted you? Then, after the situation was resolved, you discovered God's fingerprints all over the details? If so, give an example.

13. Read through Ruth 3. Compare what Naomi told Ruth to say to Boaz with what Ruth actually said to Boaz. Specifically note verses 3, 4, and 9.

    What does this tell you about Ruth's gumption?

14. What heroic qualities have you seen in Ruth thus far? Make a list.

    How did she demonstrate the qualities of an *ezer* that we saw in chapter 1?

15. What was the final result of the strength and courage exhibited in these two heroines in the book of Ruth? (Ruth 4:13-22)

    We would be missing a vital point if we saw the book of Ruth as a simple love story. In reality, this is a story of two women—two heroines—whom God used to preserve the royal line of David from which our Savior would be born. Amazing.

16. Describe any area of your life where you need to be more like Ruth—bolder for God.

LEADING LADIES

In the Old Testament, God often invited women to participate in His exploits. While the culture may have sequestered women behind the curtain as stagehands, God placed them in starring roles. Ruth and Naomi are two examples.

17. Now let's turn back even further, to the days of the great Exodus. Read Exodus 1–2:10 and note how God used the women mentioned. Explain how each one of these women showed great courage.

The Hebrew midwives

Jacobed (Moses' mother)

Miriam (Moses' sister)

Pharaoh's daughter

18. Now, turn to Judges 4:4-10.

Who was leading Israel at the time?

What were some of her duties? (Judges 4:4-6,9; 5:1)

Note how one of her duties was similar to Moses' (Exodus 18:13,15).

Deborah means "bee," and she was certainly a busy bee. (Just a note on Deborah's warning to Barak that a woman would get all the glory if she went with him into battle. She was not referring to herself, but to Jael, who is mentioned in Judges 4:21. Not exactly children's bedtime story material.)

Let's look at one more Old Testament heroine in our journey to discover God's love and plan for women. Esther was a little orphaned Jewish girl who was called out of the shadows and placed in the spotlight of God's redemptive plan. Because of her inner and outer beauty, she was chosen to be queen of a heathen nation, but with that honor a terrifying opportunity arose. The entire Hebrew nation was facing annihilation because of one jealous man named Haman. He issued a king-approved edict that, on a particular day, all of the Jews were going to be killed. Esther, whom no one in the royal court knew was a Jew, was in a position to possibly stop it. However, if she went before the king to plead for her people, and the king was not pleased with her, he could have her killed. Read her cousin Mordecai's response to her fears in Esther 4:12-14.

19. How did this courageous woman respond? (Esther 4:15-16; scan Esther 5, 7, and 8:1-10)

20. What was the outcome of her courageous move to come out of the shadows and speak to the king? (Esther 9)

21. How does this story confirm Acts 17:26?

These leading ladies of the Old Testament showed great courage as they trusted God. One thing that jumped out at me during my study of them is that while women leaders were not common, when they did appear, there was not an ounce of shock at their appearance. There is no indication they were an exception or an abnormality. The writers note the accounts of their exploits as though they were not unusual or looked down upon.

Empowered by the Holy Spirit

One thing I just love about the story of the widow who gave her two mites is the fact that she gave all she had. She may not have had much to give, but then again, Jesus doesn't need much to work with. He fed 5,000 men plus women and children with two loaves of bread and five fish, He served up robust wine with six jars of water, and He changed the world with just a handful of uneducated fishermen. All He needs is a heart that is committed to Him.

Like the widow with the two mites, you may feel you don't have much to offer, but God would disagree. You have been equipped by Him and empowered by the Holy Spirit! Let's spend this lesson taking a look at how God has equipped and empowered women to impact the world for Christ.

Before Jesus left the disciples to make His way to the cross, He promised them He would not leave them alone. Read the following verses and note what Jesus taught about the Holy Spirit.

Luke 11:11-13

John 14:15-26

John 16:7-15

1. Who was present in the room where the disciples waited for the Holy Spirit? (Acts 1:12-14)

2. Who was present and filled when the Holy Spirit descended at Pentecost? (Acts 2:1-4,14-18)

When Peter stood to explain what was happening, he announced to the gathered crowd that what they were seeing was a fulfillment of the prophecy in Joel 2:28-32. Who was included in this prophecy and in its fulfillment on the day of Pentecost?

3. One function of the Holy Spirit is that He gives spiritual gifts to believers. Read the following passages and make a list of the gifts of the Spirit. As you are reading these verses, also look for the purposes for the spiritual gifts.

Romans 12:3-8

1 Corinthians 12:4-11,27-31

Ephesians 4:11-16

The gifts overlap in various lists. Some theologians break them down into ministry gifts and motivational gifts. Some people may have more than one. But Scripture is clear that every Christian has a spiritual gift (1 Corinthians 12:11). Remember, the gifts of the Spirit are called "gifts," which means we don't earn them. They are given to us. How useful is a gift if you never unwrap it and take it out of the box?

4. Did you notice any gender specifications for the gifts? That is, did Paul say that some gifts were for women and some were for men?

5. What two spiritual gifts were women practicing in the Corinthian church as noted in 1 Corinthians 11:5?

6. What three purposes for prophecy did Paul mention in 1 Corinthians 14:3?

7. The church in Corinth was a disorderly mess. What three areas of confusion did Paul address in 1 Corinthians 14:26-35?

What did he say about the women?

But wait! Didn't Paul already mention that women were prophesying and praying in church? Let's dig deeper. If we ever sense the Bible is contradicting itself, that means we don't have a complete understanding of what God is really saying.

We must remember that much of what is written in the letters to the churches was to address specific problems. In this case, there was disorder and confusion. Women were talking in church, chatting with one another and asking their husbands questions about what was going on. The women were uneducated in the Scriptures and proper worship decorum, whereas the men had been taught these things all their lives. If Paul meant women should be totally silent, then it would mean no singing, repeating a creed, praying, making an announcement, or giving a testimony. The verse could better be translated: "Stop talking in church."

The Message says it this way: "Wives must not disrupt worship, talking when they should be listening, asking questions that could more appropriately be asked of their husbands at home. God's Book of the law guides our manners and customs here. Wives have no license to use the time of worship for unwarranted speaking" (1 Corinthians 14:34-35).

In *Christianity Today*, theologian Kenneth S. Kantzer wrote, "In 1 Corinthians 14, we are caught in an intricate interplay between quotations from a missing letter from the Corinthians and Paul's solutions to the problems the letter had raised. The verse is clearly not repeating a law of Scripture and cannot be taken as a universal command for women to be 'silent in the church.' That interpretation would flatly contradict what the apostle had just said three chapters earlier."[14]

I think of it this way. In Paul's letters, when he is addressing a problem in a particular church, it is as though we are listening to one side of a phone conversation. In light of 1 Corinthians 11:5, 1 Corinthians 14:34 could not mean total silence.

Even though Paul corrected these three areas of disorder in the Corinthian church, he did not take away the worshippers' newfound freedom, nor did he permanently silence them.

8. What was Paul's summary statement in 1 Corinthians 14:40? What was his main concern?

9. What does 1 Peter 4:10-11 tell us about the purposes of the gifts of the Spirit?

10. Read the parable found in Matthew 25:14-30 and answer the following questions.

With whom was the master pleased?

With whom was the master not pleased?

In one word, why did the servant with only one talent hide it?

In regard to your own spiritual "talents" and gifts, what can you glean from this parable?

11. One of Paul's terms for those who worked with him in ministry was "coworker." The Greek word for "coworker" is *synergos*. This word looks much like the English word *synergy*. Look up the definition of *synergy* in an English dictionary. What do you learn about the combined effort of two or more people working together?

12. If you have left your spiritual gift or gifts on a shelf and they have become a bit dusty, consider taking them down and dusting them off. What did Paul tell his friend Timothy to do with his spiritual gift that had perhaps grown a bit cold? (2 Timothy 1:6)

If you are doing this study in a group study, consider partnering with another woman and fanning your spiritual gifts into a blaze! Ask each other:

What is your spiritual gift or gifts?

How are you using your spiritual gift or gifts?

If you are not using your spiritual gift or gifts at this time, what are you going to do to change that?

13. In summary, how has God equipped women to impact the world for Christ?

Commissioned to Go and Tell

Jesus came to free us all from the darkness that descended when sin and death entered the world in the Garden of Eden. But there is an enemy who does everything within his power to keep us from experiencing the abundantly blessed, spiritually free life God intended. This week we will look through the eyes of Mary Magdalene as Jesus brought her out of the darkness and into His light.

Even though we may not have been delivered from seven demons the way our sister Mary Magdalene was, if we know Jesus as Savior and Lord, we have been delivered from the dominion of darkness and brought into the light of Christ Jesus (Colossians 1:13).

1. What does Jesus call believers in Matthew 5:14?

2. Now that we have the light of Christ living in us, what does God call us to be in 2 Corinthians 5:20?

What is the purpose or role of an ambassador?

How are you an ambassador for Christ in your everyday life?

3. An ambassador represents a person or a country. What are Christians called in 1 Peter 2:11?

4. Where is your citizenship? (Philippians 3:20)

5. Mary Magdalene is often called the "apostle to the apostles." Define the word *apostle*.

How is an apostle similar to an ambassador?

While Mary Magdalene was not one of the chosen Twelve, does she fit the description of an apostle?

Like Mary Magdalene, God saves us and then He sends us.

The least regarded by society were entrusted with the highest privilege of witnessing and relaying the most significant event in human history—the resurrection of Jesus Christ. Mary Magdalene was the first to witness the resurrection and the first commissioned to go and tell. In a culture where women were not allowed to testify in a court of law, Jesus appointed her as His key witness in the world's courtroom.

6. What two directives did Jesus give Mary Magdalene in the garden? (John 20:17)

7. How do you think the disciples felt, knowing that Jesus appeared to her rather than to Peter and John?

8. Does the fact that they did not believe Mary change the fact that she was chosen and commissioned by Jesus to tell the good news of His resurrection?

Dear friend, I hope you are catching a glimpse of a powerful truth. God still calls women out of the shadows to play leading roles in the redemption story. We should not be surprised if we face rejection.

9. What does Isaiah prophesy about Jesus? Read Isaiah 53. Pay special attention to verse 3.

10. If Jesus Himself experienced rejection, then we should not be surprised if we experience rejection as well. How did Jesus warn the disciples about future rejection? (Matthew 10:24-25)

How did He tell them to face rejection in Matthew 10:26-31?

11. John Bunyan said, "If my life is fruitless, it doesn't matter who praises me, and if my life is fruitful, it doesn't matter who criticizes me." Once we know what God thinks of us, what others think of us matters very little. What did Paul say about trying to please other people? (Galatians 1:10)

12. In Jesus' day, women were considered unreliable witnesses and not even allowed to testify in court. However, God appointed them

to be witnesses to two of the most important events in history. Consider the following:

How did Luke know the intricate details of Mary's encounter with the angel Gabriel?

How did John know the intricate details of Mary Magdalene's encounter with Jesus at the empty tomb?

Look up and define the words *testimony* and *witness*.

13. What did Jesus teach about the light we have been given? (Matthew 5:15-16)

How do we hide our light?

How do we shine our light?

Now, dear friend, what are you going to do with the light you have been given?

14. "Mary Magdalene was a woman who had nothing to offer except the shattered pieces of her broken life."[15] God could have chosen anyone, and yet, He chose Mary Magdalene to be the first eyewitness to the resurrection of His Son and the first to herald the good news. What does that tell you about the kind of people God chooses to do great exploits for Him?

Chosen for Such a time as this

I can hardly believe we are at the end of our journey together. In our final moments, I long for you to know that God has an incredible plan for you. Just like any good father, He has dreams for His precious daughters—that includes *you*. Jesus said, "I have come that they may have life, and have it to the full" (John 10:10). For any follower of Christ, that is not a life of rule-following dos and don'ts, repetitive religious rhetoric, or long-faced piety. It is a "wonderful adventure to be viewed each day on tiptoe, radiantly discovering God's Word and His ways. It is choosing to see a sovereign hand guiding, coaxing, pausing, and blessing you to the fulfillment of His purposes in your life." [16]

So let's turn our attention now to some of Jesus' final words and how we, as God's girls, can help fulfill the Great Commission in our lifetime.

1. When studying the Gospels, I was struck with how many times Jesus told His followers to "go." I have a beautiful picture in my mind of Jesus placing His hands on the shoulders of our healed and forgiven heroines, turning them around to face their futures, and pointing them forward to change the world.

   What did He tell each person to go and do? We're going to look at some of our brothers too. Look up the following verses and note when Jesus said, "Go."

   Matthew 28:16-20

   Mark 5:18-20,34

   Luke 8:47-48

   John 8:11

   From these passages, what can we surmise about what Jesus calls us to do once He has transformed our lives?

2. When Jesus healed the woman with the issue of blood, what did He push her to do? (Luke 8:45-48)

   When Jesus confronted the Samaritan woman at the well, what was she compelled to do? (John 4:28-29)

When Jesus appeared to Mary Magdalene, what did He commission her to do? (John 20:17)

3. Read and record Revelation 12:10-11. Who is the "him" in verse 11?

Why would the enemy want you to keep quiet about what God has done in your life?

4. What did Jesus tell the disciples in John 4:34-38?

Statistics show that approximately two-thirds of Christians today are women. That means there are a lot of female workers who could be bringing in the harvest. How will you respond to Jesus' call to "go and tell"?

What happened after Jesus' resurrection? Did the disciples continue with His example of valuing and respecting women as co–image bearers of God? Did they continue allowing women to walk through the doors Jesus had swung wide open? One of the best-kept secrets is the impact women had in the growth and establishment of the early church. Let's spend some time discovering the part women played.

5. At Pentecost, recorded in Acts 2, Peter preached his first sermon empowered by the Holy Spirit. How many were added to the church that day? (Acts 2:40-41)

6. How does the numbering of those added to the church in Acts 2:40-41 differ from the numbering of those who were fed during Jesus' miraculous feeding of the multitudes in Matthew 14:13-21 (note verse 21)? Matthew 15:32-38 (note verse 38)? Mark 6:30-44 (note verse 44)? Who *was not* included in the numbering of the miraculous feedings of the Gospels, and who *was* included in the miraculous conversion in Acts?

7. Read Acts 9:32-42 and answer the following questions.

How did Luke, the author of the book of Acts, describe Tabitha (sometimes called Dorcas)?

Given the circumstances surrounding this event, would you say that Dorcas was a significant or insignificant person in the establishment and growth of the church in Joppa?

8. When we are first introduced to Paul in the book of Acts, his name is Saul and he is known for persecuting and arresting Christians. Who did Saul have arrested in Acts 9:2?

What does the fact that Saul had women arrested tell you about the impact he felt they were having on the growth and spread of the gospel?

9. After Saul's miraculous conversion on the road to Damascus, God changed his name to Paul (Acts 9). On his second missionary journey, he traveled to Philippi. With whom did Paul share the gospel when he first arrived? (Acts 16:13-15)

Lydia, a woman, was the first convert on Paul's journey to Europe. Let's keep walking with Paul. Who was the second person Paul ministered to in Philippi? (Acts 16:16-18)

Who was the third person to be added to the church at Philippi? (Acts 16:29-34)

Now, describe the church of Philippi so far.

Many have suggested that Paul continued the tradition of suppressing and oppressing women. Some have even called him a "woman hater," but nothing could be further from the truth. He understood the great impact women had on the growth of the Christian faith even before he gave his life to Christ. After his conversion, Paul continued in the example of Jesus by including women in key leadership roles in the church. He recognized women as coheirs with Christ and recipients of the Holy Spirit who would partner with men to spread the gospel and build the church throughout the world.

Whom did Paul preach to in Thessalonica and Berea? (Acts 17:4,12)

10. Read the following verses and note what you learn about two of Paul's closest ministry partners: Acts 18:18-19,26; Romans 16:3; 1 Corinthians 16:19; 2 Timothy 4:19.

11. How were Philip's daughters described? (Acts 21:8-9)

12. At the end of Paul's letter to the Romans, he created quite a list of men and women who had helped him further the gospel. Of the 29 he listed, 9 were women. List each woman and what you learn about her: Romans 16:1,3,6,7,12,13,15.

From this list, what can you surmise about women involved in Paul's ministry?

13. The Greek word *diaokonos,* which we use for "deacon" (Romans 16:1), was also used when speaking of Mary Magdalene and the women who traveled with Jesus. As a review, what did Luke say about these women? (Luke 8:3)

The word "helping" can also be translated "ministering." Both are the same Greek word.

14. Paul mentioned women and their involvement in the spread of the gospel and growth of the church in other places as well. Look up the following and note who they were and what they did.

Philippians 4:3

Colossians 4:15

Paul uses the words "struggled beside me" in describing Euodia and Syntyche (Philippians 4:3 NRSV). The Greek word translated "struggle" is *synēthlēsan,* and it means "to contend, as an athlete strained every muscle to achieve victory in the games. So with equal dedication these women contended with zeal for the victory of the gospel at Philippi. He places them right alongside other workers listed in the letter."[17]

As the curtain rises to reveal part two of Jesus' story and the formation of the Christian church, the lists of women abound. In the book of Acts, Luke is careful to place women at each stage in the narrative of the church's growth and expansion: Jerusalem (Acts 5:14); Samaria (8:12); and the cities of Philippi (16:13-15), Thessalonica (17:4), Berea (17:10-12), Athens (17:34), and Corinth (18:1-2). God's female image bearers had great impact in the establishment and growth of the early church. When God said, "It is not good for the man to be alone," that included building God's kingdom as well.

15. Summarize what you have learned about the importance of women in the spread of the gospel, the growth of the church, and the support of Paul's ministry.

Read Ephesians 2:10. What does Paul call you? (So the next time someone calls you a piece of work, you can certainly agree. You are God's masterpiece.)

What does Paul tell us about one of our created purposes?

When were those specific purposes for our lives determined?

16. What do we learn in Acts 17:26 about the times and places God has ordained for us?

God has predetermined the very time and place where you live. They are no accident. You are called for such a time as this. As Rick Warren puts it, "Long before you were conceived by your parents, you were conceived in the mind of God."[18] He has specific work for you to do. It may be to impact a child, a neighbor, a community, a nation. There are no small assignments in God's eyes. We are not called to be merely spectators to what God is doing in the world but participants. He works through His people to accomplish His purposes.

Now, let's celebrate God's amazing plan as you walk in power and purpose to do all He has planned for you to accomplish!

Notes

CHAPTER 1

1. Anne Dickason, "Anatomy and Destiny: The Role of Biology in Plato's Views of Women" as quoted in Carol C. Gould and Marx W. Wartofsky, eds., *Women and Philosophy: Toward a Theory of Liberation* (New York: Putnam, 1976).

2. Bruce Marchiano, *Jesus, the Man Who Loved Women: He Treasures, Esteems, and Delights in You* (New York: Howard Books, 2008), 51.

3. Carolyn Custis James, *When Life and Beliefs Collide: How Knowing God Makes a Difference* (Grand Rapids, MI: Zondervan, 2001), 177.

4. C.S. Lewis, *Mere Christianity* (Westwood, NJ: Barbour and Company, Inc., 1952), 88.

5. Victor P. Hamilton, "The Book of Genesis, Chapters 1-17," *The International Commentary on the Old Testament*, R.K. Harrison, ed. (Grand Rapids, MI: Eerdmans, 1990), 175.

6. Note that in several Bible passages, God told men to listen to women. He told Abraham, "Listen to whatever Sarah tells you" (Genesis 21:12). King Josiah consulted the prophetess Huldah (2 Chronicles 34:22). Priscilla taught the evangelist Apollos (Acts 18:26).

7. Plato, *Timaeus,* trans. H.D.P. Lee (Baltimore, MD: Penguin, 1965), 42A-C, 90C, 91A.

8. John Temple Bristow, *What Paul Really Said About Women* (San Francisco, CA: Harper San Francisco, 1988), 5.

9. Dickason, "Anatomy and Destiny."

10. Plato, *Timaeus* in *Plato, Volume V.1: Timaeus, Critias, Cleitophon, Menexenus, Epistles*, trans. R.G. Gury (Cambridge, MA: Loeb Classical Library, Harvard University Press, 1941), 91a-d.

11. Aristotle, *Politics,* trans. Oxford University, *The Basic Works of Aristotle*, Richard McKeon, editor (New York, NY: Random House, 1941), 1.1234B.

12. Demosthenes, Adv. Neaeram, 122. Quotation by Marcus Barth, *The Anchor Bible* (New York: Doubleday, 1979), vol. 34A, 655.

13. Eva Cantarella, *Pandora's Daughters: The Role and Status of Women in Greek and Roman Antiquity*, trans. Maureen B. Fant (Baltimore, MD: Johns Hopkins University Press, 1981), 143.

14. Bristow, *What Paul Really Said About Women,* 12.

15. Leonard Swidler, *Biblical Affirmations of Woman* (Philadelphia, PA: Westminster John Knox Press, 1979), 163.

16. William Barclay, *Daily Study Bible Volume 2,* 2nd ed. (Edinburgh: St. Andrews Press, 1958), 142-43.

17. Aida Besançon Spencer, *Beyond the Curse: Women Called to Ministry* (Nashville, TN: Thomas Nelson, 1985), 56.

18. Gilbert Bilezikian, *Beyond Sex Roles* (Grand Rapids, MI: Baker Publishing Group, 1985), 60.

CHAPTER 4

1. Herbert Lockyer, *All the Women of the Bible* (Grand Rapids, MI: Zondervan, 1967), 240.

2. Sharon Jaynes, *When You Don't Like Your Story: What If Your Worst Chapters Could Become Your Greatest Victories?* (Nashville, TN: Thomas Nelson, 2021), 12.

CHAPTER 5

1. Linda H. Hollies, *Jesus and Those Bodacious Women: Life Lessons from One Sister to Another* (Cleveland, OH: The Pilgrim Press, 2007), 84.

2. Helen Keller, *The Story of My Life* (New York: Grosset & Dunlap, 1905), 23.

3. John MacArthur, *The MacArthur Bible Commentary* (Nashville, TN: Thomas Nelson, 2005), 1364.

4. Quoted in Barbara Hudson Powers, *The Henrietta Mears Story* (Old Tappan, NJ: Fleming H. Revell Company, 1957), 7.

CHAPTER 6

1. Liz Curtis Higgs, *Bad Girls of the Bible: And What We Can Learn from Them* (Colorado Springs, CO: Waterbrook, 1999), 229.

2. A more complete telling of this story is found in my book *Becoming Spiritually Beautiful: Seeing Yourself from God's Perspective* (Eugene, OR: Harvest House Publishers, 2009), 187-89.

CHAPTER 7

1. James B. Hurley, *Man and Woman in Biblical Perspective* (Grand Rapids, MI: Zondervan Publishing House, 1981), 72.

2. Josephus, *Against Apion,* 2.201.

3. Michael Griffiths, *The Example of Jesus* (Downers Grove, IL: InterVarsity Press), 132.

4. James, *When Life and Beliefs Collide*, 39-40.

5. Ibid., 167.

1. M.L. del Mastro, *All the Women of the Bible* (Edison, NJ: Castle Books, 2004), 270.

CHAPTER 9

1. Loren Cunningham and David Joel Hamilton, *Why Not Women?* (Seattle, WA: YWAM Publishing, 2000), 116.

2. Kenneth Barker, gen. ed., *NIV Study Bible* (Grand Rapids, MI: Zondervan Publishing House, 1995), 1500-1501 (footnote on Mark 5:22).

3. Hollies, *Jesus and Those Bodacious Women*, 44.

CHAPTER 12

1. Susan Haskins, *Mary Magdalene: Myth and Metaphor* (New York: Harcourt Brace & Co., 1993), 63.

2. Mary R. Thompson, *Mary of Magdala: Apostle and Leader* (New York, NY: Paulist, 1995), 47.

3. "Mary Magdalene: The Hidden Apostle," Biography, prod. Bram Roos, A&E Television Networks, 2000, videocassette, as quoted by Liz Curtis Higgs in *Mad Mary* (Colorado Springs, CO: WaterBrook, 2001), 143.

4. Higgs, *Mad Mary*, 142.

5. Neal W. May, *Israel: A Biblical Tour of the Holy Land* (Tulsa, OK: Albury, 2000), 244.

6. Higgs, *Mad Mary*, 150.

7. Frank E. Gaebelein, ed., *The Expositor's Bible Commentary*, vol. 8 (Grand Rapids, MI: Zondervan, 1992), 584.

8. Matthew Henry, *Matthew Henry's Commentary of the Whole Bible,* vol. 5 (1706; reprint, Peabody, MA: Hendrickson, 1991), 672.

9. Higgs, *Mad Mary*, 251.

10. Carolyn Custis James, *Lost Women of the Bible: The Women We Thought We Knew* (Grand Rapids, MI: Zondervan Publishing, 2005), 187.

CHAPTER 13

1. Erwin and Rebecca Lutzer, *Jesus, Lover of a Woman's Soul* (Carol Stream, IL: Tyndale House Publishers, 2006), xii.

2. Carolyn Custis James, *The Gospel of Ruth* (Grand Rapids, MI: Zondervan Publishing House, 2008), 66.

BIBLE STUDY GUIDE

1. Gilbert Bilezikian, *Beyond Sex Roles* (Grand Rapids, MI: Baker Academic, 2006), 17.

2. W.E. Vine, Merrill F. Unger, William White Jr., *Vine's Complete Expository Dictionary of Old and New Testament Words* (Nashville, TN: Thomas Nelson Publishers, 1985), 73.

3. John MacArthur, *The MacArthur New Testament Commentary: Romans 1-8* (Chicago, IL: Moody Press, 1991), 13.

4. Beth Moore, *Breaking Free: Making Liberty in Christ a Reality in Life* (Nashville, TN: Thomas Nelson Publishers, 1985), 160.

5. Erwin Lutzer and Rebecca Lutzer, *Jesus, Lover of a Woman's Soul* (Carol Stream, IL: Tyndale House Publishers, Inc., 2006), 11.

6. *Reflections of Hope Bible Study* (Colorado Springs, CO: International Bible Society, 2009), 17.

7. Diane Dempsey Matt, *The Reluctant Traveler* (Colorado Springs, CO: NavPress Publishing Group, 2002), 155.

8. "Single-Person Households in the United States from 1960 to 2020," Statista, accessed April 12, 2021, https://www.statista.com/statistics/242022/number-of-single-person-households-in-the-us.

9. Mark Rutland, *Streams of Mercy* (Ann Arbor, MI: Servant Publications, 1999), 39-40.

10. Peter Kreeft, *Three Philosophies of Life* (San Francisco, CA: Ignarius Press, 1989), 99.

11. Kenneth L. Barker and John R. Kohlenberger III, *NIV Commentary, Volume I: Old Testament* (Grand Rapids, MI: Zondervan Publishing House, 1994), 292.

12. Carolyn Custis James, *The Gospel of Ruth* (Grand Rapids, MI: Zondervan Publishing House, 2006), 66.

13. William D. Mounce, *Mounce's Complete Expository Dictionary of Old and New Testament Words* (Grand Rapids, MI: Zondervan Publishing House, 2006), 128.

14. Kenneth S. Kantzer, "Proceed with Care," *Christianity Today*, October 3, 1986.

15. Bruce Marchiano, *Jesus, the Man Who Loved Women* (New York, NY: Howard Books, 2006), 104.

16. Michael Richardson, *Amazing Faith: How One Man Spent His Life Taking God at His Word: The Authorized Biography of Bill Bright, Founder of Campus Crusade for Christ International* (Colorado Springs, CO: WaterBrook, 2001), 76.

17. Victory C. Pfitzner, *Paul and the Agon Motif: Traditional Athletic Imagery in the Pauline Literature* (Leiden, Netherlands: Brill, 1967), 120.

18. Rick Warren, *The Purpose Driven' Life* (Grand Rapids, MI: Zondervan Publishing House, 2002), 23.

BIBLE TRANSLATIONS USED

ACKNOWLEDGMENTS

Many men and women have influenced my life and challenged me to walk over to a fresh canvas and read the Gospels with new eyes:

Naomi Gingerich, who challenged me years ago to reconsider my own ideas about women in ministry.

Campus Crusade, whose mission is to reach out to women all around the world through the Magdalena project and subsequent film, *Magdalena: Through Her Eyes.* Specifically, Jenny Steinbach, Gail Ratzlaff, and Bill Sims, who caught the vision of how the Magdalena help women all around the world understand just how much God loves and cherishes His female image bearers.

My Girlfriends in God, Mary Southerland and Gwen Smith, who constantly cheer me on with encouraging words and lift me up with powerful prayer.

My editor, Kathleen Kerr, who always takes what is good and makes it better and best.

My heavenly Father, who gently, tenderly, and sometimes sternly kept pointing me back to His Son, Jesus Christ, when I asked the hard questions regarding how He really felt about women.

Jesus Christ, who continually invited me to take a closer look at how He treated women against the backdrop of societal, political, and religious prejudices of His day.

The Holy Spirit, who confronted me, convicted me, and finally convinced me.

My husband, Steve, who daily holds up the mirror of God's Word for me to see myself as a dearly loved, cherished child of God, and encourages me to help other women see themselves as the same.

ABOUT THE AUTHOR

Sharon Jaynes has been encouraging women through ministry for over 25 years. From the time she met Christ as a teenager, she fell in love with God's Word and has had a passion to equip women to live fully and free. Her passion is to encourage and empower women to walk in courage and confidence as they grasp their true identity as a child of God and a coheir with Christ.

For ten years Sharon served as Vice President of Proverbs 31 Ministries and co-host for their daily radio feature. She is the author of 24 books with Harvest House, Moody Publishers, Baker Books, Multnomah Publishers, and Thomas Nelson. She has also written numerous magazine articles and devotions for publications such as *Focus on the Family, Extraordinary Women, Decision, Crosswalk.com,* and *In Touch.* Sharon is a frequent guest on radio and television programs such as *Revive Our Hearts* with Nancy Leigh DeMoss, *Family Life Today* with Dennis Rainey, and *Focus on the Family.*

Sharon currently writes for Proverbs 31 Ministries' Encouragement for Today devotions, and teaches at their She Speaks conference.

Sharon is the co-founder of Girlfriends in God, Inc., a non-denominational ministry that crosses generational, denominational, and racial boundaries to bring the body of Christ together as believers.

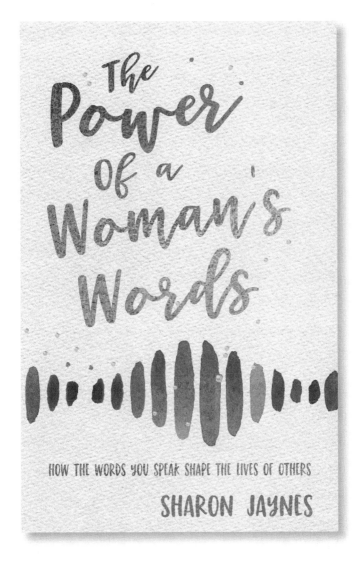

The Power of a Woman's Words

Of a

Woman's

Words

HOW THE WORDS YOU SPEAK SHAPE THE LIVES OF OTHERS

SHARON JAYNES

Your words have the power to shape and influence those around you. If you desire to use your words to build up rather than tear down, to encourage rather than discourage, to cheer rather than jeer, you can learn to control the mighty force of the tongue.

SILENCING
THE LIES THAT
STEAL YOUR
CONFIDENCE

enough

SHARON JAYNES

Bestselling author of *The Power of a Woman's Words*

Sharon Jaynes exposes the lies that keep women bogged down in guilt and shame. Learn to recognize and replace the lies you've told yourself and find confidence and rest in your identity as an imperfect—but wholly redeemed—woman of value.

To learn more about Harvest House books and
to read sample chapters, visit our website:

www.harvesthousepublishers.com

HARVEST HOUSE PUBLISHERS
EUGENE, OREGON